JoAnne King

Jupiter:
the Preserver

Jupiter: the Preserver

BY

ALAN LEO

Being the substance of a Course of PUBLIC LECTURES
delivered before the ASTROLOGICAL SOCIETY *in the
months of October, November and December,* 1916

WITH AN INTRODUCTION

SAMUEL WEISER
New York
1973

SAMUEL WEISER INC.
734 Broadway
New York, N. Y. 10003

ISBN 0-87728-020-7
Library of Congress Card No. 72-16452

Printed in U.S.A. by
NOBLE OFFSET PRINTERS, INC.
New York, N.Y. 10003

SYNOPSIS

	PAGE
Introduction - - - - -	vii
Lecture I. JUPITER AS PRESERVER—The Symbolism of Jupiter and its connection with other Symbols.	1
Lecture II. JUPITER AND THE GREAT LIFE WAVE—Comparison of Jupiter with the Trinity.	31
Lecture III. JUPITER AND THE PERSONAL AURA—The connection of Jupiter with Substance and the Material World.	57
CONCLUSION: The Planetary Rays.	77
Note by the Acting Editor of " Modern Astrology."	80
A WORD TO THE FEW.	82

FOREWORD

. . . . In what way the student of Astrology sees the working of planetary influence in man, while yet regarding him as essentially FREE, will be set forth in the following pages. <u>The Wise Man rules his stars</u>, the <u>Fool obeys them</u>.

. . . . May these lectures prove helpful and useful to those sufficiently awake to understand them, those who have begun to realise something of the great truth that <u>CHARACTER IS DESTINY</u>.

These concluding sentences from the Forewords to the two previous Volumes of this Series sufficiently indicate the spirit in which the author has conceived the present work, and in which he would desire that the reader should approach it.

London, N.W., 11/9/1917.

There is the same relation between natural and judicial or judiciary astrology, as between physiology and psychology, the physical and the moral. If in later centuries these were degraded into charlatanry by some money-making impostors, is it just to extend the accusation to those mighty men of old who, by their persevering studies and holy lives, bestowed an immortal name upon Chaldea and Babylonia? Surely those who are now found to have made correct astronomical observations ranging back to " within 100 years from the flood," from the top observatory of the " cloud encompassed Bel," as Prof. Draper has it, can hardly be considered impostors. If their mode of impressing upon the popular minds the great astronomical truths differed from the " system of education " of our present century and appears ridiculous to some, the question still remains unanswered: which of the two systems was the best? With them science went hand in hand with religion, and the idea of God was inseparable from that of his works.

H. P. BLAVATSKY IN "*Isis Unveiled*," i 267.

INTRODUCTION

WHEN the annual course of public lectures first delivered before the Astrological Society in January-March 1915 was originally contemplated, it was not intended to go beyond a "popular series" that would include lectures on the influence of Mars, Saturn, and Jupiter. Nor was it intended that any particular 'label' attached to the influence of each should be considered as exclusively applying to that planet alone. For the first lectures "*Mars: the War Lord*" was chosen as a suitable and appropriate heading, having regard to the Great War then in its earliest stages, and some stress was laid on the fact that the influence of MARS on the Desire-Nature acted as a *sower of seed* for future reaping. Naturally therefore a year later followed a course of lectures on "*Saturn: the Reaper*," in which the relation of Saturn to the fruit of action was dealt with. And lastly, in the autumn of the same year, a course dealing with the influence of JUPITER as the Preserver—forming the contents of the present book.

But in order to avoid any misconception in the

minds of those who may approach Astrology for the first time through these lectures it may be necessary to mention what is well known to astrological students, regarding the sense in which these 'labels' have been used in connection with the planets MARS, SATURN, and JUPITER.

In practical Astrology, THE SUN is the beginning and end of all planetary influences. The solar orb is viewed as the centre of our system, the physical or outward glory of the Essential Influence or Intelligence radiating throughout the Whole Solar System. From this centre comes forth a trinity of Intelligence which is Creative, Preserving, and Dissolving (or regenerative). This TRINITY is reflected in each planetary sphere of influence, having a physical planet as its centre denoting an active manifestation of the creative, preserving, and regenerative principles.

In the manifesting vibrations of JUPITER we may trace more of the preserving than of the creative or dissolving influence; but it is only because the one is active, while the other two appear to be latent. This apparent anomaly may be explained by reference to the trinity of zodiacal signs over which a planet presides. For instance JUPITER governs the signs *Sagittarius* and *Pisces*, and is exalted in the sign *Cancer*. In the human family the influence of Jupiter is mainly social, charitable, and religious. In the sign Cancer, Jupiter's influence is prolific, preservative and harmonious; in

INTRODUCTION ix

Sagittarius, it is creative; and in Pisces dissolving or regenerative;—but presiding over the trinity of signs as a whole it is decidedly preserving and harmonising.

In the case of SATURN the dissolving or regenerative attributes appear to be uppermost, but the preserving and the creative are also there, no matter how latent. The dissolving or regenerative influence appears to be more manifest in *Capricorn*, owing to the changeableness of the sign, while the creative seems to be more evident in *Libra*, and the preserving more pronounced in *Aquarius*.

With regard to the planet MARS we may find the creative side active through the sign *Aries* the preserving instincts more active through *Scorpio* and the regenerative more operative through the sign *Capricorn*.

Astrology is expressed through the numbers one, three, and seven, and the manifestation of three outlets of influence is shown in every symbol, affecting the mind, emotions, and the physical conditions. Each planet has its own primary influence, together with a sub-influence of the other planets. Thus THE SUN represents spirit, life, and vitality,—three aspects of the One Light universally manifested. THE MOON represents soul, mind, and instincts; while THE EARTH (typified by the ascendant) represents bodies that are fixed and stable, or active, or balanced. These three, symbolised by ☉ ☽ ⊕, are again blended with other symbols, giving a wider and fuller interpretation, or an extreme ex-

JUPITER: THE PRESERVER

pression of a fundamental influence; for instance we may arrange these symbols as follows:

$$\begin{array}{ccc} ♀ & ♃ & ♆ \\ ☉ & ☽ & ⊕ \\ ♂ & ♄ & ♅ \end{array} \Bigg\rangle ☿$$

and find the whole resolved into the symbol of the planet MERCURY, containing the influence of the three in one,—the symbol of the Adept.

MARS and VENUS are two extremes of one influence on the life side of manifestation: Venus is the creative influence and Mars the generative. SATURN and JUPITER are two extremes of one influence on the form side of manifestation. Jupiter is the preserving and subjective side of that which manifests as the objective and concretive influence of Saturn; and, in this sense, Jupiter is the *less limited physical*.

To those who desire to understand the interweaving influence of the planets there is no better plan than to consider SATURN and JUPITER as rulers over the lower and higher physical conditions, and MARS and VENUS as rulers of the lower and higher emotional nature. Then the three states of the human being can be summed up in MERCURY as the perfect blending of the physical, emotional and mental nature in the truly HUMAN being.

INTRODUCTION

Had another course of lectures been given in connection with the present Series, the influence of the planet MERCURY: THE MESSENGER would have been treated of in a similar manner to that in which Mars, Saturn, and Jupiter have already been dealt with.

An archaic Manuscript—a collection of palm leaves made impermeable to water, fire, and air, by some specific and unknown process—is before the writer's eye. . . . The first illustration is a plain disc, ○. The second in the archaic symbol shows a disc with a point in it, ⊙—the first differentiation in the periodical manifestations of the ever-eternal Nature, sexless and infinite, or potential Space within abstract Space. In its third stage the point is transformed into a diameter, ⊖. It now symbolises a divine immaculate Mother-Nature within the all-embracing absolute Infinitude. When the horizontal diameter is crossed by a vertical one, ⊕, it becomes the Mundane Cross. Humanity has reached its Third Root-Race; it is the sign for the origin of human Life. When the circumference disappears and leaves only the +, it is a sign that the fall of man into matter is accomplished, and the Fourth Race begins.

From " The Secret Doctrine," pp. 31, 34.

Jupiter:
the Preserver

Jupiter: the Preserver.

LECTURE I.

SYNOPSIS.—Jupiter as Preserver—The Symbolism of Jupiter and its connection with other Symbols.

BEFORE we consider the nature and influence of the planet Jupiter it will be well to consider the symbology associated with the planetary bodies, because we may find a true interpretation of each planet's influence by noting its symbol and the relation it bears to other symbols.

The symbols of the five planets, with the Sun and Moon, are derived from combinations of the glyphs of the CIRCLE, the CRESCENT and the CROSS, which are the accepted symbols to represent *spirit, soul, and body*. These with their meanings are as follows:

Circle,
 Crescent,
  Cross,

Symbol	Name	Meaning	Associated Symbols	
☉	SUN	Spirit—life	♀ VENUS	♂ MARS
☽	MOON	Soul—mind	♃ JUPITER	♄ SATURN
⊕	EARTH	Body—matter	combined in	☿ MERCURY

The associated symbols on the life side are Venus and

JUPITER: THE PRESERVER

Mars, *Circle* and *Cross;* and on the form side Jupiter and Saturn, *Crescent* and *Cross*. Uranus and Neptune, the two modern planets, are the higher octaves on the life and form side, for which we have no ordinary symbols and we use the arbitrary symbols ♅ and ♆ for them.

To understand something of the vibrations of each planet we must know the department of nature it is said to govern, and whether it is related more to the life or the form side of manifestation; and when viewing the planets as creative principles we should understand their rank and position in the Celestial Hierarchy. *We must, however, remember that we cannot separate life from form on any plane of manifestation, but can only see where the life forces are dominating the form or where they are being dominated by them.*

Life-in-Form

JUPITER is probably the highest expression of the form side of manifestation we can hope to understand, and as such it represents an ideal beauty—and exquisite organisms of every conceivable form until the beatific vision is contemplated. On the form side of manifestation Jupiter's influence is known to be harmoniously expansive, while that of Saturn is steadily contractive; and our experience has confirmed the idea that Jupiter expands the form to its highest capacity of refinement, and therefore

Expansion and Contraction

tends to produce an ideal in abstraction; while with Saturn the ideal is reached in concrete exactitude and particularisation.

To contrast these two formative expressions of planetary influence, SATURN favours the expression of mind through form in sculpture, architecture, and physical science; that is to say, in the building of a perfect structure: JUPITER, in beautifying, in the decoration and adornment of the edifice when raised, and in the highest philosophy or adoration that can be expressed through any structure. Through Saturn's influence an expression of mind is made that takes shape and form in dense matter, while Jupiter's influence is exhibited in the abstractions of the mind that are turning away from concrete matter. The influences or vibrations of both Saturn and Jupiter have organising tendencies, Saturn ever tending to shape in detail, or by forming a fresh series of limitations, Jupiter organising in principles, causes and communities. Saturn as a separative influence fashions the structure in the individual, Jupiter as a unifying influence moulds communities and nations. Jupiter is the revealer of hidden and secret things, and so far as the form side of the universe is concerned Jupiter unfolds what Saturn binds or hides. Jupiter influences the unfolding of all seeds and preserves them until they are able to express the life concealed within in a fitting environment

*The Individual
and
the Community*

until that life can unfold, blossom or ripen. Saturn on the other hand restricts and limits what might be an over-rapid growth until the *time limit* of its expansion is exhausted. In the physical form Saturn ever tends towards isolation and the separateness of the individual, Jupiter on the other hand tending to bring out all that is sociable, co-operative and harmonising.

To help our understanding of Jupiter's nature and influence we may study the symbol which has *always* been associated with this planet, the crescent over the cross— ♃.

Every human being is a Soul or Consciousness, which through the medium of the mind is an ever changing mode of expression or attitude towards its Real Self, the spirit; symbolised by the changing ☽ to ☉ in all its phases; and towards that which is not itself, the not-self symbolised by the + or physical ⊕. Each soul is passing through the " cycle of necessity " for the purpose of gaining a more refined and permanent individuality (♄) that will survive the long pilgrimage on the Cross of matter in the lower or material worlds. In its incipient stage the soul of every human being as instinctual consciousness is symbolised by THE MOON (☽), for it is full of changing moods and is lacking in continuity, very forgetful, easily affected externally and careless of authority; like the Moon it is vaporous, changeable and colourless. The action of

What is a Human Being?

LECTURE I.   5

MARS on the Moon awakens the energy that is associated with the sensuous side of consciousness and attracts material towards the gratification of the senses regardless of consequences. SATURN'S influence compresses and limits the vapourings of the lunar tendencies, and JUPITER expands what Saturn has previously made stable or firm.

The Soul coming into manifestation as a human being, may, from a materialistic standpoint, be compared to a fine film of the rarest substance. Under the influence of the Moon (considered apart from other influences), as an entity it is at first colourless, young and inexperienced, but between the limitations and contractions of Saturn's influence, and the higher organisations and expansions of Jupiter, it becomes *tempered* by the vibrations or colourings of the planets—literally expressed as varied experiences produced by many environments.

We are taught that every human being is in essence an immortal spark of the divine flame, "a divine fragment"; and every soul, for the purpose of expression in the worlds of form, is composed of the finest film of the subtle supersensuous matter which pervades all space. It has its normal existence on higher planes of nature than the physical, but for the purpose of expression in denser bodies such as the physical, vehicles are required through which it can manifest. Therefore, just as the soul is

JUPITER: THE PRESERVER

the vehicle for the manifestation of spirit from a higher plane, so is the physical body the vehicle for the soul's expression on the physical plane; and later on, we shall have to demonstrate the relationship of Jupiter to these vehicles. Every separate entity, or individual soul, has been derived from a great over-soul, and although divine in the beginning of its soul-birth it was destined to descend into denser planes of matter in order to *win*, through personal effort and merit, its conscious immortality.

There are three distinct aspects of every soul; its involution into the lower and denser planes of matter, during which period it is only conscious,
Three Stages and not self-conscious; its self-conscious aspect on the lower planes where experience is gained of the value of material expression; and finally the super-conscious aspect when evolving upward out of the lower planes of denser matter.

The involving aspect is symbolised by the Moon in its connection with and circulation through the zodiacal circle, which contains the prototypes of all
In, and Out objective forms, each of the signs giving a permanent colouring to the animal instincts of the form. The Moon in its relation to the zodiac, collecting the influences or impressions caused by its aspects with the planets, awakens self-consciousness, the realisation of individuality and the distinct impression of separateness in an outer world. The withdrawal

LECTURE I.

comes when the soul endeavours to rule the stars through self-control and by working consciously with the higher modes of planetary influence. In the earlier stages of spiritual unfoldment the soul is irresponsive, unsympathetic, and indifferent. In the later stages the soul is intensely responsive, sympathetic and compassionate, lending itself to every cry of pain with understanding and charity.

To some extent we may map out the various stages and aspects of a soul's growth and by means of the symbology of Astrology exercise an intuitive insight into hidden causes. But we can never learn the truths Astrology has to teach us with regard to the human soul, until we have ceased to criticise a nativity in the spirit of fault-finding, using the same critical faculties to discriminate and to synthesise the *whole* horoscope. For until we have that attitude of wise discrimination we cannot fully understand the lessons a soul may have to learn or the life experiences (summed up in the word karma) it is working through at that particular time in its evolution.

The Staircase of the Soul

In a horoscope we may see the line of least resistance, the karmic disabilities, and the nature of the environment.

So far as the Soul can be depicted by symbology alone, apart from the colouring of actual experience, we may trace the general stages as follows:—

JUPITER: THE PRESERVER

☽, *plus* The Zodiac :—Involution into the physical.
☽, „ ♂ & ♄ :—Struggle and storm, critical stage.
☽, „ ♀ & ♃ :—Expansion of creative powers.
☽, „ ♅ & ♆ :—Occultism or mysticism.

When a child is born into the physical world, the *whole* of the horoscope is instantaneously photographed and impressed on the plastic brain,—not one or two planets or zodiacal signs alone,—although the planetary vibrations may be dumb notes so far as the physical vehicle is concerned, as in the case of idiots : "*An idiot or natural fool is one that hath had no understanding from its nativity.*" All *sensible* beings, however, must respond more or less to planetary influences, otherwise they are dead to the gods or angels. Animals respond to the zodiacal influences according to their nature, and not to the planets in their wider range of influence,[1] for the vibrations of the planets are *intelligent* vibrations affecting the body through the *human soul*.

If a human being can only respond to the lunar influences he is little more than a lunatic. And since it

What is Insanity? is affirmed that one person in every 600 in Britain is either a lunatic or insane, it becomes of interest to enquire what constitutes the difference between sanity and insanity, or lunacy? The Moon plus Mars alone, in certain positions in a horoscope, without modifying

---

[1] In the case of very highly specialised domestic animals there may be some exceptions to this general rule : see Nos. 094 and 781 in *Notable Nativities*.

influences, causes insanity or madness, the intellect having departed, leaving behind nothing but the animal nature. Sanity is the result of Saturn's cooling influence upon the Moon; the word is derived from *sanus* meaning whole or sound—having the regular exercise of reason.

The Moon plus Saturn gives sanity through self-control; the vapourings and inconstant influences of the ever-changing Moon are ordered or organised by the cooling influence of Saturn. The Moon rules the grey matter of the brain, and Saturn gives its composition; or in other words, the Moon collects the material and denotes its functional quality and Saturn arranges, composes or compounds it. The limitations of the soul are laid down and defined by Saturn for organising purposes in the lower worlds, but if Saturn alone affected the soul it would never escape the bondage of these limitations, they would bind it for ever.

☽ + ♄

Given a soul that has had imposed upon it the greatest bondage a physical brain and body can endure, where shall we look for the method of its return to a purer atmosphere? This is a question we should be able to answer in the present course of lectures under the heading of Moon plus Jupiter. When the weight of experience in the physical world, while bound to the cross of matter, has limited the consciousness to that real state of individualisation

"Where is my Mother?"

where it can stand alone and realise its isolation as an individual, it then, figuratively speaking, does what all young children do on finding they are lost, it cries out—"Where is my mother?"

The Mother of the Soul
Jupiter is the great Mother of the Soul, the Preserver of all things in time and space, and if we symbolise Jupiter as the Over-Soul in space and Saturn as the individual soul in time, it is only to show the form aspect of the eternal substance which these planets represent. We cannot now enter into a metaphysical explanation of Jupiter's connection with Vishnu, or the second person of the divine Trinity, who is the Preserver of everything in the universe that is subject to time and space, but we may explain that the great mother of humanity is symbolised in the second aspect of the Trinity, representing a dual manifestation of the Supreme Intelligence as Love and Wisdom, and from that Wisdom all intelligent beings are born. We have unfortunately to use many words and materialise many ideas before we can understand the nature and effect of planetary influence with regard to human souls; and, short of intuition, which is an inner perception of things, we are obliged to demonstrate these ideas in physical terms to our mind and senses. The only demonstration of the Soul that our senses or everyday reason can accept is the *mind*, which is either involved in the senses, or is the abstract mind, which is ruler over them;

LECTURE I.

and this is why it is a question of response and identification as to the stage we symbolise by the particular division of the Crescent and the Cross. There is only one Supreme Spirit—God—The First Logos ; but there are many lesser spirits or gods. For us as humans there is only one Over-Soul; but there are many lesser souls. There is only one Substance, but many forms and divisions of dense and fine matter or vehicles for the soul.

The Moon, which is said to be a substitute for a mystery planet, (that is to say a planetary sphere whose vibrations are too rapid and subtle for us to respond to at present), has primary importance over each personal expansion of an individual centre ; and although the individual concretion may be retained as personal temperament under the influence of Saturn, the cream or aroma of each personal life is drawn into and preserved in the aura of the ego under the influence of Jupiter. In one of the Standard Text Books[2] we learn that Jupiter is the planet of expansion and that every individual is encircled by an aura, which comes directly under the vibrations of Jupiter. We expand and gradually increase the size and quality or contents of that aura during each earth life, more, or less, according to our development; and whether in objective manifestation in the physical world

The Aura

---

[2] *How to Judge a Nativity*, p. 35 (Third Edition.)

12 JUPITER: THE PRESERVER

or in the heavenly or subjective worlds, this aura is our own and contains our whole history, the result of the past and the possibilities of the future; and in this sense Jupiter is the ruler over the celestial or immortal part of the *higher* physical consciousness or "*Prana*" manifesting through the physical body.

Metaphorically speaking, the symbology of Astrology is an unfoldment of the circle from its central point, or the full radiation of the Sun, the fiery ☉ —☽— ✛ centre of our solar system surrounded by the circle marking the boundary of its spiritual life, the aura of the Solar Logos or Supreme Intelligence in whom we have our life and being, as Solar atoms, or " Divine Fragments "; and each symbol evolved out of the point and the circle is the expression of a special manifestation. The Crescent, taken as the Moon of our Earth, symbolises the ebb and flow, or expansion and contraction, of that aura, and denotes an increasing fulness of expression in a condensed substance, as from a gaseous fiery condition to a cooler manifestation in a watery element. The Cross symbolises the dense manifestation of that aura in physical atoms and molecules, as the axes or lines of growth in crystals.

The symbol for an advanced human being, one who has control over his mind and senses, is that of the 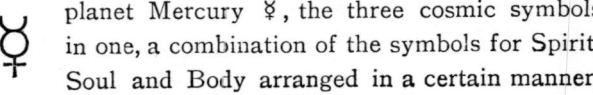 planet Mercury ☿, the three cosmic symbols in one, a combination of the symbols for Spirit, Soul and Body arranged in a certain manner,

LECTURE I. 13

the Crescent being uppermost, implying a *human* intelligence, which although not complete until a full expression of Spirit, Soul and Body is achieved, is nevertheless in process of becoming a complete expression on the physical plane. The divine seed, symbolised by the point in the centre of the circle, is unfolding its inherent qualities. The Crescent placed uppermost denotes the advanced state of the soul, receiving and reflecting light from above.

This symbol of the three in one, ☿, implies that Mercury is the essential nature of every human being, the yolk within the egg, over which the **The Messenger** preserving influence of Jupiter broods **of the Gods** until the complete unfoldment of the spirit is reached. The importance of Mercury's influence in every nativity is well known to astrologers, who never judge this planet *alone* or apart from the influence of the other planets, until man is an adept. Mercury is the Messenger of the Gods, the Interpreter, unfolding all that Jupiter contains infolded. We cannot know the true nature of any planet's influence unless it be interpreted through Mercury, the planet of true Soul knowledge, the planet of *Soul*, not brain, memory.

This reference to Mercury requires some explanation with regard to Jupiter's relationship with that planet. In the zodiac Jupiter and Mercury alone govern ♃ & ☿ the mutable cross, and are partners, so to speak, in the rulership over the Mutable signs and the elemental essence therein represented. In the order of the signs Mercury rules the third and sixth houses, and Jupiter the opposite ninth and twelfth houses, and in this respect they are related to the intuitional and inspirational mind and to the sympathetic emotions as crucified on the human cross. Mercury brings soul knowledge as an inheritance from former births, <u>Jupiter brings wisdom gained by experience through expansion of human consciousness in form.</u>

The Seven Principles The seven planets are the indicators of the seven Principles which constitute the universe; they are divided into what may be termed higher and lower principles, or cosmic and human. The seven planets are not separate and distinct influences unconnected with each other; on the contrary each planetary influence contains within itself the whole seven subordinated to the one which its symbol denotes and concealing the other six, which are only manifested when in conjunction or some potent aspect that liberates one or more of them. The four lower principles of each planet are connected with the elements, or elemental essences, and therefore affect physical things through the objective elements air fire, water, and earth, and the vehicles of consciousness connected with them, known as the intuitional, mental, emotional, and physical bodies (or sheaths).

Just as the circle of the zodiac is a complete whole and

homogeneous in itself, with twelve divisions, so are the planets a complete whole in the aura of the Sun with seven divisions. As said in *Esoteric Astrology*, there is but One Ray coming through the Sun, and this is broken into seven rays through the planets, which seven are again broken into millions of rays, each separate form of matter being ensouled by one of these broken rays.

The One Ray

Each planet has a dual expression of itself, a higher and lower, a positive or negative, or male and female manifestation, as shown by the two signs of the zodiac over which it has an influence in consciousness. If each planet had a separate and distinct influence of its own, Astrology would be much simpler to define than it is to the concrete mind. Essentially, each planet has its own special influence, which may be discovered on knowing its universal influence as a vibration affecting certain types of matter or certain principles. But when we come to particulars, we find that in the material world the sub-influences of the planets are more active than the major influence, the material world being the plane of activity.

Dual Expression

In a general sense Mars may be said to represent an acid, positive or masculine mode of expression; Saturn an alkaline, negative or feminine mode; while Jupiter may be thought of as the "salt of the earth," the universal soul of things, the seed or germ of all

Acid, Alkali, and Salt

material things. It would however be incorrect to say that Mars alone governs all acids, Saturn all alkalies, and Jupiter all salts; although the tendency in each of these planets is toward those conditions of matter. Astrologers consider the whole of the muscular system of the human body as under the influence of the planet Mars, the bones under Saturn, and the blood and cell-life under Jupiter; but it is also true that *all* the planets affect the muscles and the bones and the blood in a general sense. Truth and beauty may be and are, Jupiterian aspects, but there are also Martian and Saturnine types of truth and beauty.

The fact to be grasped is that there is ONE UNKNOW-ABLE LIFE, *both transcendent and immanent*, and ONE UNIVERSAL SUBSTANCE ; and through these ALL life and form are manifested by the combining and compounding of planetary influences. Therefore symbolically we make the Cross a neutral representative symbol of matter and the Crescent a neutral symbol of the Soul; and then by combining the Cross and the Crescent we find either matter or the soul predominating as the case may be, and trace as many combinations arising out of them as is possible for the purpose of particularisation. *If students of Astrology will make the known and accepted symbols the basis of their Esoteric Astrology, they will come far nearer to the heart of the science than those who ignore them.* The symbol of the Sun

Meaning of Symbols

LECTURE I.

☉ is the one symbol from which all others are derived, and the point in the circle, representing the unit or figure 1, symbolises the mathematical basis of Astrology which will make it the exact science it should be, if only we are careful not to be too rigid in our personal particularisations.

With this idea ever present in our mind we may consider that on the form side of things JUPITER governs the blood and the seed in the human organism. The life of the body is the blood and the life of the blood is the air. The life of the nerves is the *prana* or vital force. When blood and nerves are healthy the whole organism is healthy; and this is why JUPITER and MERCURY, governing the common or mutable signs, nourish physically or mentally the whole organism specially ordered and controlled by these two planets. They cannot act alone, however; for without co-operation of the motive energy and muscular apparatus of MARS, the stability and bony structure of SATURN, and the fleshy substance and venous system of VENUS, the blood would not flow through the system as a whole. The reason why one planet cannot act alone in a human organism is due to the disintegrating or deadening influence of each when taken separately. The bones require tendons and ligaments, and without the intervention of Mars or muscular activity the salts in the blood would tend to ossification and to accumulate

No Planet singly

JUPITER: THE PRESERVER

deposits such as uric acid, stone, gravel, rheumatism, etc. The muscular system on the other hand acting alone, and unrestrained by Saturn, would tend to inflammatory conditions, extravagant expenditure of energy, and overwork. It is the 1 or "I" in us that is the point around which all the influences and tendencies are moving in the circle of our auric life, and it is owing to the circulation of the blood and of the vital and nervous fluids, and their relation to the aura, that Jupiter is finer and more subtle in its influence than Saturn or Mars.

Because we cannot depend upon one planet's influence alone, we temper the stars within us, and cannot afford to consider any planet higher or lower than another. Jupiter's influence over the blood may be quite as malefic as that of Saturn over the bones, the salts, and the concrete mind; for we may have diseases of the blood causing tumours or cancer, or apoplectic tendencies; and while the vices of Saturn may be greed or miserliness those of Jupiter cause gluttony and wasteful extravagance. The virtue of Jupiter is harmony and the vice of harmony is hypocrisy,—a sham harmony. The principles of the planetary influences as affecting humanity are neither virtues nor vices; they are qualities common to all who tune themselves to them, for they are latent in every human being. They are: MERCURY, Reason; VENUS, Affection; MARS, Energy; SATURN, Endurance; and JUPITER, Preserva-

Tempering the Stars

LECTURE I. 19

tion. The contractions of Saturn and the expansions of Jupiter when properly understood are but cyclic movements of the life in relation to finer or denser matter; the ebb ♄ and flow ♃ of the neutral ☽. The decay of old age or disease is but the absorption of the finer elements of the body into the more interior or subjective states. We are more limited in the external expression than in the internal. The marrow in our bones is limited more than the blood in our veins, because of the texture or quality of the binding material; but in essence there is only one substance in the body over which the influence of all the planets presides, and that is the seed of life.

Each planet has a secret to reveal to those who are intuitive enough to discover it. The divine seed falls into the soul of a human being and grows into a human life through the material vehicle of the body. The seed apparently dies in the effects of its activity; it was the cause of all the manifested life on the denser planes of matter. It does not suffer an utter death, however; it merely yields up its divine essence or life in order that a self-conscious life in matter may result; it dies to live, so to speak; in other words, it dies to the higher and finer planes of matter to expand that life in and through the limitations of the physical world. It is Jupiter's mission to preserve the essence of the seed, and in preserving its divine aroma it savours

"The Moon, Sin, and Soma"

all that it touches. The body is the sepulchre in which our King is buried. Saturn binds it, and at the same time offers the means of its redemption through purification. Jupiter is the revealer of the secret of the mystic words—"The Moon, Sin and Soma." The Moon is the Soul in its infantile state of innocence, before it has awakened to a sense of separateness. It falls from this heavenly state of innocence, is tempted by the serpent of desire, and emerges from the circle only to be bound to the Cross or wheel of necessity through ignorance.

Sin is the attachment to that form which is lower or denser than itself, the becoming inferior by the limitations of coarser matter; and the symbol of sin is ♄ Saturn, or Satan, the tempter through the carnal mind which binds it to the cross of matter, the concrete physical body. The Soma juice is the spiritual wine or "living water" which effects the redemption or resurrection of the soul now risen into the finer planes, having abstracted the personal self and mingled freely with other selves and surmounted the cross,—♃. In the Bible we have the pictorial representation in Adam, Jesus, and Christ; the animal-, human-, and God-man. The degradation of man is through the malefic side of the planets MARS and SATURN (astrologically interpreted as a personal abuse of certain principles which in themselves are in no way evil); but without this degra-

A Definition of Sin

LECTURE I.   21

dation the Soul could not unfold its power or quality and would remain neutral to the world of self-consciousness. The redemption of man is through the benefic side of VENUS and JUPITER, love and beauty, which restore the soul to its innocence together with a self-conscious knowledge of the value of good and evil, love and hate, the Self and the not-Self.

We cannot dissociate Jupiter from Mercury any more than we can separate the Moon and the higher physical influence of Jupiter from Saturn, **Jupiter and Mercury** or Venus from Mars; they are inseparable pairs alternately ruling the objective and subjective parts of the one reality they conceal. Mercury is associated with the breath of life, the air we breathe and the lungs by which we breathe, as the *messenger* of the Gods, those Gods who rule the planes of Ether in the heavenly worlds. Jupiter is associated with the blood, arterial and venous, and its vapours or life.

As already stated, each planet has its active and its passive house, and has also its active and passive qualities hidden within itself. There **Active** are two principles into which all things **and** **Passive** are resolvable; the male, active, expansive and disseminative; and the female, passive, compressive and receptive. Jupiter's relation to the blood may be discovered by a careful study of the sign Pisces, the passive or form aspect of Jupiter's influence. Pisces is the mutable sign of the watery triplicity and represents the universal solvent cosmically, and in the microcosm the life blood of animals and men. Aquarius represents life in its highest and lowest forms on the positive side; and Pisces, which is life on the passive or form side, therefore denotes life in form, from the great Avatars to fishes, from the Avatar Matsya to the sea anemone; for in this sign are hidden the secrets of Moon, Sin and Soma. It is the sign of submission, passivity and yielding, or all that is *involuntary*.

The Fishes in the sign Pisces are pictured as swimming in opposite directions, symbolising life descending into mortality and life ascending into im-

The Sign Pisces mortality; and in this aspect Jupiter, its lord and ruler, represents life and death (that is, change and mutability—for there is no actual death), or expansion and regeneration. In human life it often symbolises failure and self-undoing; but out of the failure comes the realisation that man's life is a vapour or an essence to be distilled from the dregs of his emotions. In the spiritual world it represents the Saviours of men who came to save those who are "lost" (that is, lost in the maze of the material world), to redeem them through the universal solvent, Wisdom-Love. Cosmically it represents the plane or field of Varuna, the God of Waters; the astral and subjective planes. In its lowest aspect it symbolises the gray world filled with the ghosts and shades of men; and in its highest aspect those who have drunk of the living waters of eternal life and renounced its glory for the helping of men.

If we knew the real nature of the blood that ebbs and flows through our physical bodies we should know Jupiter and all that its sphere indicates; but we cannot see the active principle of the life-blood coursing through our veins and arteries, although we know that it is really a vapour, an essence, or an ex-pression of the air globules received through the lungs and changed by a subtle alchemy in the crucible of the heart. There are three distinct processes in all actions connected with the planetary vibrations and the physical body; such as the ebb and flow or integration and disintegration of the form and of the life-principle affected by the changing form; the expansion and compression of the lungs, the inspiration and expiration of air through the breath, and the systole and diastole of the heart-beat—with the balance between the two in each case. What happens with each indrawn breath is an *incarnation* of the creative principle; and it is the same with every muscular effort, and every exercise of the intelligence or of the feelings.

Ebb and Flow,— Incarnation and Reincarnation

The Crescent in relation to the Cross has three distinct aspects in its waxing and waning influence. First unattachment, in its free circulation round the cross (☽); second, attachment to the cross

Crescent and Cross

♄); and third, detachment or liberation (♃). The vapourings of the Moon's ebb and flow are attracted to the earth by the condensation of Saturn, where the fixation point is reached and the volatility of the Moon's influence is lost; symbolically, the soul is bound to matter—♄. That which has been apparently lost is only concealed, however, even as the fluidic condition of water is hidden in ice. Jupiter is the revealer of secret and hidden things, and by a subtle transformation the essential elements are transfused into higher and finer bodies than the material, which is under the concrete Saturn, and ascend into that region of our being known as the Soul; and then that which has been dead and buried as Saturn has risen as Jupiter.

The relation of the Mutable Cross of the zodiac to the planets Mercury and Jupiter reveals the spiritual side of Astrology to those who love the esoteric.

The Mutable Cross

The three crosses of the zodiac, Cardinal, Fixed and Mutable, represent the head, trunk and limbs or extremities of the human form. The trunk is the base, to serve which the limbs and head or five points exist. In this sense the highest become the servants; and, as the dual nature of the mutable signs denotes, they serve both the highest and the lowest. The hidden point is at the centre of the Cross; it is the mystery point around which the dual influences of the other four points are turning. It is the point of the germ seed which either

LECTURE I.   25

gravitates to the wheel of necessity or ascends through the spiral of a regenerate and eternal life. We cannot dwell too long on this aspect of Jupiter's powerful influence in relation to the mutable cross, although in another lecture of this series we shall consider the connection between the inbreathing of the nostrils and the generative principle, but we may make one final allusion to the sign Pisces, which represents the feet of man and also his *understanding*.

Pisces is the last sign of the zodiac, if we may be allowed to make any sign first or last. It denotes the outflow of life and its corresponding return. Taurus, Aries, Pisces There must be an inflow before there can be an outflow. We cannot stop to show the relationship of the sign Cancer to that of Pisces, but we may observe that as the pure springs of water that flow from the mountains into the valleys are the distilled rains that drop from the heavens, so is the milk of the human breast the source of nourishment to the growing life. We have not advanced to that knowledge which reveals the fact that each sign of the zodiac, as a representative of the pure elements, symbolises a living form; the earthy signs stimulating the physical life, the electric current of life entering TAURUS, the vital organs, through the fixed signs and travelling through the body to the knees, Capricorn, and then returning to Virgo, which rules the Solar Plexus. The astral or mental-emotional life begins with the sign

ARIES, ruling the two hemispheres of the brain, and floods the sensitive organs of the cardinal signs; and passing through the sign Scorpio, the critical point, returns the current of emotion through the sign Pisces, the sign either of failure or of emancipation. The breath enters the lungs (Gemini), and stimulates the whole of the nervous system and motor organs through the mutable signs which end with the sign PISCES and the feet which stand upon the earth.

Saturn compresses the life of the elemental essence, and Jupiter expands it; these are the two modes of all manifesting life, compression and expression, inbreathing and outbreathing.

Each sign of the zodiac is an apostle silently witnessing to the truth of the heavenly as well as of the physical man. The zodiac is Adam Kadmon, the **Adam Kadmon** heavenly man, and each division of the circle shows the progress of life through forms; the fixed signs found or establish the life on a whirling centre or wheel in the body by a rotary vibration, and liberate force in active changeful feeling connected with the sensory system, finally transmuting its quality in the mutable signs over which the planet Jupiter presides in the wider sphere. The air inhaled by the lungs is ruled by the mutable sign Gemini, and is absorbed by the globules of blood and carried throughout the body. The zodiac, contracted in ourselves, the microcosm or little man, is a bubble on the

LECTURE I.

ocean of life, which we expand into a living globe of most wondrous construction filled with living forces, a globe constantly contracting and expanding during each earth life.

Life is so simple that a child might understand it, and yet so complex that the greatest scientists are puzzled by its complexity; although after all is said there is only one life expressed in many forms. The air that enters our lungs passes through the crucible of the body, and there it has to undergo the transformation of the martian and saturnian vibrations before it can find the equilibrium or balance which the sign Libra denotes, and finally pass out through the MAN, or manas, sign Aquarius. In the breath and the blood is concealed the secret of manifested life in the physical world—"For the life of the flesh is in the blood": *Lev.* xvii, 11. Every act in life is a sowing of seed ($♃$), and hunger ($♂$) is the motive power of all our sowing. We reap in the concrete physical as we have sown, and every compression or contraction is a reaping ($♄$). We live as we express, for all life is a seeking to reveal ourselves in a bud or blossom that shall bring a fruitful life.

One Life, Many Forms

The ethers of space are concealed in the air we breathe and transformed into blood globules with their circling motion round the body. When the outlet of the spiral sign Aquarius is reached the ethers

The Waters of Lethe

are liberated in a spiral of thought, free of personal emotion, into the soul (manas). But if desire or emotion still binds the self to the things of earth they pass again into the waters of the sign Pisces by incarnations few or many, until the true liberation of manhood is reached. The arterial blood flowing through our system is symbolised by the sign Sagittarius, which, in common with all the positive signs, is a spiral influence; and the venous blood by the negative or passive rhythmical sign Pisces, in which Venus is exalted. The venous blood in the human system has to find its way back to the place from which it started, and it is the vaporous essence given off by the circulation of the venous blood as it returns to the sign Pisces, and all that it represents through its ruler Jupiter as human essence that makes a lasting impression upon the human aura and its KARMA.

Concerning this word Karma of which we have had and shall have so much occasion to speak we read in the Theosophical "Glossary" that the meaning of **Karma** this word is "physically, action; metaphysically, the Law of Retribution, the law of cause and effect or Ethical Causation. It is the power which controls all things, the resultant of moral action, or the moral effect of an act committed for the attainment of something which gratifies a personal desire. There is the karma of merit and the karma of demerit. Karma neither punishes nor rewards, it is simply *the one* Universal Law which guides unerringly and so to say blindly, all other laws productive of certain effects along the grooves of their respective causations. When Buddhism teaches that 'karma is that moral kernel (of any being) which alone survives death and continues in transmigration' or reincarnation, it simply means that there remains nought after each Personality but the causes produced by it; causes which are undying, *i.e.* which cannot be eliminated from the Universe until replaced by their legitimate effects, and wiped out by them, so to speak, and such causes—unless compensated during the life of the person who produced them with adequate effects, will follow the reincarnated Ego, and reach it in its subsequent reincarnation until a harmony between effects and causes is fully re-established. . . ."

"Our notions of solids, liquids, and gases are derived from our experiences of the state of matter here upon this Earth. Could we be removed to another planet, they would be curiously changed. On Mercury water would rank as one of the condensible gases; on Mars, as a fusible solid; but what on Jupiter?

"Recent observations justify us in regarding Jupiter as a miniature sun, with an external envelope of cloudy matter, apparently of partially-condensed water, but red-hot, or probably still hotter within. His vaporous atmosphere is evidently of enormous depth, and the force of gravitation being on his visible outer surface $2\frac{1}{2}$ times greater than that on our earth's surface, the atmospheric pressure, in descending below this visible surface, must soon reach that at which the vapour of water would be brought to its critical condition. Therefore we may infer that the oceans of Jupiter are neither of frozen liquid nor gaseous water, but are oceans, or atmospheres, of *critical* water. . . . . Jupiter is neither a solid, a liquid, nor a gaseous planet, but a *critical* planet, composed internally of associated elements in the *critical* state. . . . ."

Quoted in the SECRET DOCTRINE, ii 144.

[*The sense in which the word 'critical' is here used is almost identical with that associated with the words common and mutable in Astrology. The critical condition is the boundary line between solid and liquid, or between liquid and gas, neither one nor the other but partaking of the nature of both.*]

LECTURE II.

SYNOPSIS.—Jupiter and the Great Life Wave—Comparison of Jupiter with the Trinity.

"The Seven Beings in the Sun," says the *Secret Doctrine*, "are the Seven Holy Ones, self-born from the inherent power in the matrix of Mother-Substance. It is they who send the seven principal Forces, called Rays, which at the beginning of a Universal Night will centre into seven new Suns for the next Life-cycle. The energy, from which they spring into conscious existence in every Sun, is what people call Vishnu, which is the Breath of the Absoluteness."

Seven Holy Ones in the Sun

There is a Unity underlying all things, which a faith in the Stars reveals, although it may not be intelligible to our physical senses. From the Seven Holy Ones in the Sun, who are self-born, we may trace reflections through the various subtle planes of our Universe down to the seven principles in man. If it were possible for us to know of other Solar Systems than our own in the immeasurable space in which they

Seven Principles

float, we are given to understand that we should find the same method of expression running through them all so far as their UNITY is concerned.

From the Absolute, the source of all life and form, there arises the one Breath which moves through all universes, and that energy is known as Vishnu, or the Supreme Being, who is at once the Creator, Preserver, and Dissolver (or Regenerator) manifesting through every universe.

1,—
3,—
7,—
12,—

In Astrology as in other systems of abstract thought we speak of the ONE—the Sun; the THREE—Sun, Moon, and Earth; the SEVEN—the planets; and the TWELVE—the signs of the zodiac. These apparently arbitrary divisions in a manifested universe are apt to be perplexing to those who are not familiar with the inner teaching of Esoteric Astrology. The difficulty in comprehending the various divisions often arises through the duplication of the three, by reflection, and the dividing line between them, making the seven; and this is further complicated when we study states of consciousness and their corresponding forty-nine (7×7) planes of matter, and their many combinations.

The planes on which our ordinary humanity is evolving are three—the physical, the emotional, and the mental; these are summed up in the physical world as the plane of action. Then there are two on which super-

The Three Planes

LECTURE II. 33

human beings function, known as the spiritual plane, and the plane of wisdom. These are the five planes on which consciousness evolves until the human merges into the divine. Above these are two planes known as the spheres of divine activity, which at present are beyond our knowledge.

The particular point of interest to students of Astrology is that each plane is presided over by a great Intelligence, a God, an Angel, a Deva,—it does not matter which term we may be inclined to use so long as we think of the plane in which this Being works as *the field of his consciousness*. Above and beyond the seven planes there is always the Logos or God over the whole system or universe, who is revealed to us as a trinity. He, the supreme intelligence, manifests a part of Himself, but a part remains ever unmanifested. This is the divine law of all universes; the supreme Ruler over each system of worlds reflects the ONE manifested centre in the Unity of the absolute and unknowable source of All manifestations; and all we can say of *THAT* is that it IS; everything comes from and returns to *THAT*.

The Supreme Ruler

In our endeavour to understand the universe in which we live and have our being we confine our studies to the Solar System, the centre of which is the Sun, symbolised by the point and the circle—☉. From the point in the centre of space, enclosed in the outer ring, arise three

The Trinity

34   JUPITER: THE PRESERVER

lines symbolising the trinity familiar to all religions, and philosophically representing the *Self*, the *Not-Self* and the *Relation between them*;[1] and we may here state that astrologically speaking Jupiter is the planetary representative of the RELATION. From the standpoint of the spirit, this trinity is expressed as *Will, Wisdom,* and *Activity,* the Divine Triad. The Solar Logos, symbolised to us by the Sun, is expressed in this trinity as Father, Son and Holy Spirit, or in ancient religions as Shiva, Vishnu, and Brahma,— reflections of the Universal Trinity: Jupiter, the Relation, Wisdom, and Vishnu, are all correspondences. In the Kabalistic system of thought the three divine aspects of the Logos are known as Kether, Chokmah, Binah.

These three are beyond our understanding from any material standpoint, and the subject can only be approached by deep meditation and reverence;

F.C.M.

but we may find some correspondence in the world of form in connection with the three qualities latent in the FIXED, CARDINAL and MUTABLE signs of the Zodiac, and this correspondence we may trace later; this is symbolised by a figure similar to that just given, in which however the three equidistant radii have their ends joined by three chords, thus forming

---

[1] The three lines in the symbol should be equidistant and should reach the circumference of the circle. The printers have used the nearest type available, but it will serve to convey the idea.

LECTURE II.

an equilateral triangle enclosed within a circle with lines connecting the centre to each point of the triangle.

For us it is useful to know that these aspects of the Logos impose certain qualities on matter. The First Cause of all manifestation, while expressed
Rare on the life side in three aspects, also affects
and
Dense the Universal Substance or matter in which the manifestation is made, for there can be no expression of life without a fitting form to contain it. In every world there is a life and a form, combined in distinctive units of consciousness. We may think of the Sun and of the seven planets rooted in the Sun as life expressed through very fine and rarefied forms; and of the earth on which we dwell as dense matter, becoming more and more dense as we proceed in thought to the centre of the earth. The Earth has finer grades of matter surrounding it in the air and ether. The Moon, between the planetary spheres and the earth, is related to the earth and to the outer limits of the earth's sphere, the zodiac, by the finer and grosser types of matter surrounding the earth, translating the qualities of the signs of the zodiac through her node.

Following the Hermetic teaching "As above, so below," we find a reflection of the divine aspects and
the qualities of matter in the
Will, Wisdom, Activity zodiac, the WILL aspect in
the Fixed signs, the WISDOM
aspect in the Mutable signs, and the ACTIVITY aspect

in the Cardinal signs. These three crosses in turn affecting the world's progress by the slow precession of the equinoxes.

Considering now the planetary rulership, the Fixed Signs as a whole are under the influence of SATURN, the Tamasic Guna or stable quality reflecting
F.C.M. the Will aspect in the material world as
desire. The Mutable Signs are under JUPITER, reflecting the Wisdom aspect as *knowledge* in the material world. The Cardinal Signs are under MARS, reflecting the activity aspect in *action* and *generation*.

These we find again reflected in the triplicities, with the Airy Signs as the pivot or turning point between spirit and matter, and as the influence that
F.E.A.W. relates the elemental essence to the qualities,—that is, the qualities of the triangle to the cross. The Fiery Signs in the abstract are under the dominant influence of THE SUN and MARS, the Watery Signs under JUPITER and the Earthy Signs under SATURN, as nominal rulers for certain periods. These are the three great influences running through all life and form and tending to produce respectively Mobility, Rhythm, and Stability. By an arrangement into which the decanates of each sign enter we have seven distinct types arising out of the three fundamental aspects and qualities of matter, in each of which is a definite type of life expressing itself in a particular form ;

LECTURE II.   37

and these seven are again multiplied by seven, and so on, until an almost infinite variety of forms are produced. In order to trace the influence of Jupiter through the seven divisions, we may set out a part of this arrangement as follows:

QUALITIES AND TRIPLICITIES.

Signs.	1. FIXED	2. MUTABLE	3. CARDINAL
Quality	Stability	Rhythm	Mobility
Aspect of Consciousness	Will	Wisdom	Activity

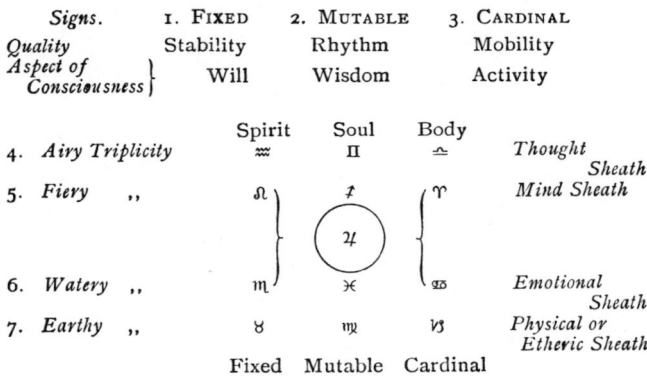

		Spirit	Soul	Body	
4.	*Airy Triplicity*	♒	♊	♎	*Thought Sheath*
5.	*Fiery* ,,	♌	♐	♈	*Mind Sheath*
6.	*Watery* ,,	♏	♓	♋	*Emotional Sheath*
7.	*Earthy* ,,	♉	♍	♑	*Physical or Etheric Sheath*
		Fixed	Mutable	Cardinal	

The AIRY signs of the zodiac are links with the macrocosm. The Fiery and Watery signs represent the microcosm; and the Earthy signs are related to the physical or material world.

The process of involution and evolution may be astrologically symbolised by a series of seven crosses.

Involution, and Evolution
Three of these are concerned with the downward arc of involution; one, the middle cross, is concerned with the struggle between Spirit and

38 JUPITER: THE PRESERVER

Matter; and then three with the upward arc of evolution. The first three are ruled by the Fixed, Cardinal, and Mutable signs on the angles as follows:—

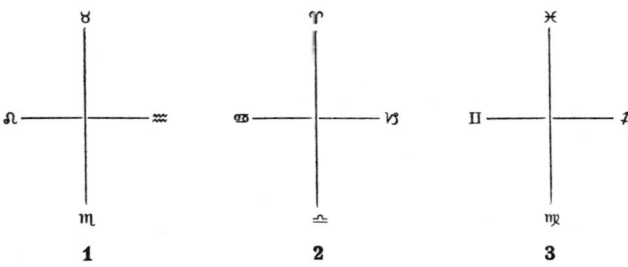

      1   **2**   **3**

The first is concerned with the First Round of a chain of globes, in which the first act of Creation is at work through the formless fiery Breaths, the Lords of Fire, Divine Flames, known as the " Fiery Lions, Lions of Life "—the Life and the heart of the Universe concerned with awakening the Will in the monad of man.

The second is the plan of the Second Round of a Chain of Seven Globes and the third of the Third Round. In these three Rounds *qualities are imparted* to matter. The Fourth Round is engaged in the work of struggle, forming manifold relations between Spirit and Matter; it is symbolized by the Fixed Cross, whose influence remains for many millions of years as we count time, thus :—

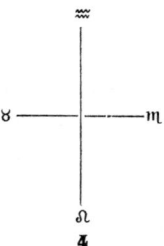

The three evolutionary crosses are then symbolised as follows.—

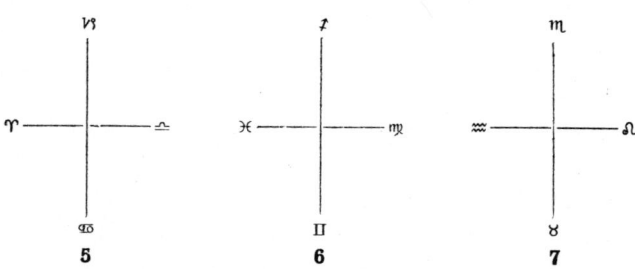

The Earth lives through seven Rounds, and in each Round there are seven Root Races on each Globe, with seven sub-races to each root race. We 4-4-5-5 cannot enter into all the elaborate details of these Rounds, Races and Sub-races, but it may be accepted that the more civilised portion of humanity is now in the Fourth Round, Fourth Globe, Fifth Root-Race, and Fifth Sub-Race. The fourth cross is the permanent cross for the whole Round, in which appear seven Root-Races and forty-nine Sub-

40 JUPITER: THE PRESERVER

Races. The fifth cross is now active for the fifth Root-race, and also for the fifth Sub-race of the fifth root-race. It is under the dominant influence of the planet MARS as ruler of the Racial ascendant—*Aries*. We may now repeat these three crosses forming a diagrammatical picture of the point in evolution at which we are now arriving:

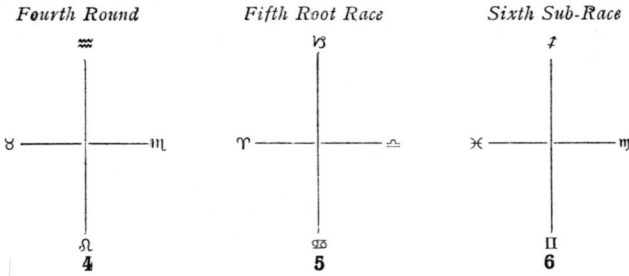

Cross No. 5 represents evolution on the earth at our present stage, the "Kali Yuga," or Iron age, with the Cardinal signs on the angles. The next age will be represented by the Mutable signs on the angles when the influence of the great God Vishnu will be supreme and the planet Jupiter will rule the midheaven and the ascendant instead of, as now, Saturn and Mars (♑ and ♈).

While it would afford a basis for some interesting speculation to trace the influence of the three aspects of the Solar Logos through the **Shiva, Vishnu, Brahma** various planes of matter as beautifully expounded in such

LECTURE II. 41

books as *A Study in Consciousness*, we must be content with the observation that in our astrological studies we find the divine trinity reflected in some mysterious fashion in the planets Saturn, Jupiter, and Mars, representing Shiva, Vishnu, and Brahmā in terms of will, wisdom, activity, and reflected through the Fixed, Mutable, and Cardinal signs of the zodiac as Desire, Cognition and Action. The upper part of our diagram (Fifth Root Race cross), which is the ordinary map of the zodiacal signs, shows at a glance that Saturn, Jupiter and Mars govern the heavens above the earth (with the exception of Libra—Venus—for the seventh house) which represents the MACROCOSM, while every element is represented and every quality also in the houses of Stability, the tenth and eleventh; Rhythm, the ninth and twelfth; and action, the first and eighth.

Before a world can be formed for human habitation, we are told, it has to be built from the three elemental worlds which are pouring downward in involution into the more dense and concrete worlds. SATURN'S influence begins by an action which corresponds to the cosmic process of "digging holes in space," and by a mighty rotary motion. Gravity is finally produced, matter is solidified, and the mineral kingdom eventually appears. Then follows the work of JUPITER in drawing out and organising the latent life of the mineral by powerful attractive vibrations, and the vegetable world

Mineral,
Vegetable,
Animal

is finally perfected. Lastly the influence of MARS brings into existence the animal kingdom, and in the higher animals the stability of Saturn and the rhythm of Jupiter are combined with the strength and mobility of Mars. The world is then ready for the incoming of the human family, and out of these three primary influences of Saturn, Jupiter, and Mars, by combination and permutation, much specialization of life and form is produced, and to their primary action we are indebted for our permanent physical, astral or emotional, and mental atoms and finally our higher consciousness. The work of Saturn has made it possible for us to have stability, not only through the bones and ligaments of our physical bodies, but also through the purification of our emotions, with permanent modes of feeling and desiring as well as a sound concrete practical mind that will lead us to concentration and meditation. The work of Jupiter has supplied us with a blood stream in which our Egos may live and contact the physical world through race, nation and family life; also with a higher physical or subjective mind and the possibility of expansion through a finer and more ethereal atmosphere. The work of Mars has given us our excellent muscular system through which we may obtain skill in action, as well as a strength of mind that enables us to express devotion to the object of our affections. In one sense these three influences are far below the human scale, and yet in another they are far beyond us. For all

LECTURE II.   43

practical purposes they seem to be more closely connected with the sub and super human states than with the definitely human, and yet we know that without their aid there could be no human progress.

In our first course of lectures, *Mars: the War Lord*, we traced the descent of Spirit into the material world from Aries to Libra, and so on; and in the next course, *Saturn: the Reaper*, we amplified these ideas. We have now to trace the influence of Jupiter in our human evolution. Normally all souls extract permanent experience out of the six signs from Aries to Libra, and these are well known to the majority of students, exhibiting as obedience under Taurus, adaptability under Gemini, sensitiveness and sympathy under Cancer, loyalty and faith under Leo, and discrimination between the real and the unreal under Virgo. In Libra a state of balance has to be reached before the Ego is ready to pass out of the plane of the senses into that of the higher mind, when, balanced and ready to stand alone, the work of regeneration through the Scorpio influence may be safely attempted; for then a man begins to reverse his spheres, to live for the many rather than for the one—himself. The pleasures of the senses and the lusts of the flesh latent in the sign Taurus must be crushed out before the regenerative influence of Scorpio can liberate the pure vital fluid that is no longer to be used for generative purposes, but for those of the creative. The diffusiveness of the discursive

[Marginal note: Man]

mind of Gemini must be balanced in Libra before the creative mind can be used or knowledge changed to Wisdom. The personal sensitiveness of Cancer with its sympathy for its own must also be changed for that inner sensitiveness that will allow for the expansion of Jupiter, exalted in this sign, to turn the sensitiveness inward to the astral or higher emotional plane. The abounding life of Leo with its wonderful " Prana " and self-reliance must be transmuted into loyalty to the higher Intelligences who touch the heart of the man who aspires for freedom. And then comes the real discrimination that knows the true from the false, the real from the unreal, which leads to a balanced state that ascends the spiral staircase leading to the real man. There must be no struggle between the higher and the lower, the desires and the action, when Jupiter the Preserver begins his work of emancipation through a widening consciousness; for all who touch the vibrations of Jupiter come into the presence of God, though they know it not.

Before we can understand the particular phase of consciousness connected with the planetary sphere of Jupiter, we must learn something of **The Second Life Wave** what is known to occultists as the "Second Life Wave." From the FIRST LOGOS—a centre of energy containing in Himself inseparate a dual substance, the eternal root of consciousness and the eternal root of matter—emanates the SECOND, in whom the twain appears as two aspects, Spirit-Matter; and from Him arises the THIRD, or Universal Mind.

It is the Eternal Substance that is manifested through the SECOND LOGOS which becomes the substratum of matter in the various grades of its manifestation.

In the third volume of the *Secret Doctrine*, page 585, we are told:—" Absolute eternal motion, Parabrahman, which is nothing and everything, motion inconceivably rapid, in this motion throws off a film, which is Energy, Eros. It thus transforms itself to Mulaprakriti, primordial Substance which is still Energy. This Energy, still transforming itself in its ceaseless and inconceivable motion, becomes the Atom or rather the germ of the Atom, and then it is on the Third Plane. . . . We always begin on the Third Plane; beyond that all is inconceivable." As we believe there is some relation in the material world between Jupiter and the Second Logos, the indivisible duality or Second Person of the Trinity connected with the evolution of form, we may conceive that so far as human evolution is concerned the special influence of Jupiter consists of the reproduction in matter of the archetypal ideas in the Mind of the Logos; these ideas are taken by the Builders and they guide the preparatory stages and direct the definite shaping in the later. Nature-spirits work under their inspiration and perform

The Second Person of The Trinity

the actual task of moulding matter on the physical plane.

The archetypes reflected from the Mind of the Logos through the signs of our earth's zodiac, are again reflected outwards in due course for the ♐ and ♓ guidance of His agents, the images falling from plane to plane until they arrive at their destination—figuring first as ideas, and then as astral forms, ere taking on a physical semblance. This influence is most active in the mental and fiery sign Sagittarius, giving rise to religion, philosophy and science, in aspiration, meditation and speculation, in which the matter of the mental sheath becomes more and more expansive. In the sign Pisces the emotional sheath is expanded through the feelings and emotions, temperate and harmonious, but accentuated for good or ill in Cancer and Scorpio.

Throughout the whole of the outpouring of the Second Life Wave the goal sought is the perfecting of forms wherein the life of the Logos can be expressed. We can now see why Jupiter is connected with beauty, ceremony, and the perfection of forms. Working with Saturn the forms become more and more stable on the downward cycle, till when the denser forms are reached they lose plasticity in gaining stability; but on the upward arc they evolve greater stability and *regain* plasticity, while at the close of our human evolution our forms will

Stability with Plasticity

LECTURE II.

have extreme stability wedded to perfect plasticity—a union that at first glance seems impossible. One of the first problems that meets the esoteric student is how to reconcile the limitation or contraction of Saturn with the plasticity or harmonious expansion of Jupiter, in each sign of the zodiac as well as each house in a horoscope. In connection with the idea of Jupiter and human evolution the esoteric student has been told that:

1. The forms in all kingdoms are built by Beings ranging in Intelligence from superhuman to subhuman.
2. These Beings, although evolving on this earth and its related planes, are on a line of evolution which does not normally intermingle objectively with the human.
3. There is a Monadic evolution *downwards* in the three elemental kingdoms; its nadir is the mineral kingdom; its evolution is *upwards* in the vegetable, animal, and animal-man kingdoms.
4. The Monad has passed through states of evolution on other globes before reaching our earth.
5. The Monad carries on its activity along seven lines or Rays, each distinguished by its own characteristics.
6. In the evolution of form the Monad descends through the three elemental kingdoms to the mineral and then re-ascends through the vegetable and animal to the human.

These ideas we may set out as follows : (p. 48)

The work of the FIRST LIFE WAVE is that of preparing the materials for a Solar System out of the Primordial Substance; that of the SECOND LIFE WAVE is the evolution of forms; and the work of the THIRD

MONAD.

Downward	Level or Plane	Upward	
First Elemental Kingdom ↓	FORMLESS	Man—*Permanent Sheath* ↑	
Second Elemental Kingdom ↓	FORMED	Man—*Mental Sheath* Animal-Man Kingdom ↑	{ *Germinal Mental Sheath*
Third Elemental Kingdom ↓	ASTRAL	Animal-Man Kingdom Animal Kingdom ↑	{ *Emotional or Astral Sheath*
Etheric Gaseous Liquid Solid } Mineral Kingdom ↓	PHYSICAL	Animal-Man Kingdom Animal Kingdom Vegetable ↑	{ *Physical or Food Sheath*
↓	MINERAL (Nadir)	↑	

LECTURE II. 49

LIFE WAVE is to meet the forms as they are evolving upwards and to fill each form with an embryonic, individualised consciousness or SELF.

Considering the system in its totality, we have first the Logos and the three aspects, or the Trinity of God the Father, God the Son, and God
Our Solar System the Holy Spirit. Then there are the Seven Spirits before the Throne of God, who stand immediately below the Trinity of the Solar System and are charged severally with the care of seven Planetary Chains, each presiding over one of these vast evolutionary schemes. These also form the Seven Rays of the Solar system; each scheme of evolution proceeding along one of the Rays, at the head of which stands its own Planetary Logos.

It is not possible, neither is it wise, for us to seek to go into minute details with regard to the Rays at present, although astrology is directly con-
The Planetary Rays cerned with an understanding of our evolution through them. Briefly, there are seven streams of tendencies, each distinguished by a dominant characteristic, including in their seven groups all things whatsoever in our world. These streams are called "Rays," and they are often represented by the colours of the solar spectrum, as no names for them have been given to us. Everything in the phenomenal world belongs to one or other of these Rays, and the lines of evolution run down the separate

JUPITER: THE PRESERVER

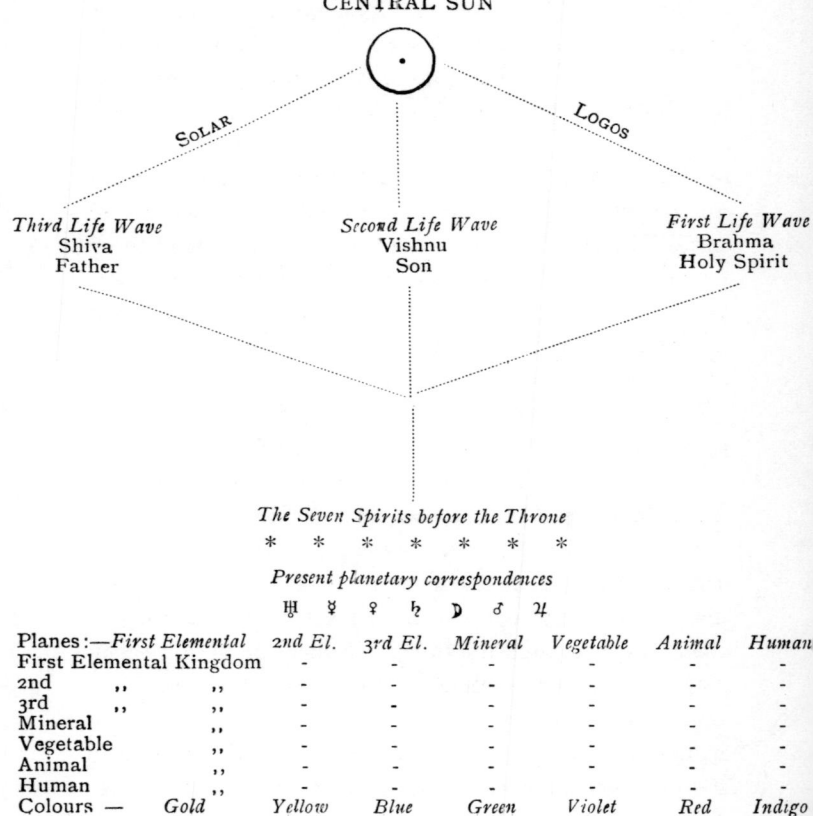

LECTURE II. 51

streams, not crossing from one into another in any kingdom below that of man and only rarely in his. The differences between them are differences of quality, *i.e.* of rates of vibration. They might be figured as running vertically, side by side, down through the planes represented as horizontal; each elemental kingdom would thus have its seven divisions, as would each of the four physical plane kingdoms. When a man is said to be born under a particular star it really means that he is born into its corresponding Ray. We cannot be sure that we have the corresponding planet for each Ray quite correctly, but so far as our information concerning our present evolution goes, the planetary correspondences are as given above. It will be seen that we have placed Jupiter under the seventh Ray; there is a special reason for this which we shall endeavour to explain in our third lecture.

So far as the Rays are concerned, apart from any planetary correspondence, each Ray is composed of seven sub-rays, every colour in the solar **Sub-Rays** spectrum being present in each Ray, but dominated by the main colour of the Ray: *e.g.* in the Violet Ray, the sub-rays will be violet-violet, indigo-violet, blue-violet, green-violet, yellow-violet, orange-violet, red-violet; and so on, continuing with each of the other rays.

This gives us forty-nine sub-rays, each distinguished from its fellows by difference of quality, *i.e.* by its

vibratory possibilities. These 49 sub-rays
49 × 49 again sub-divide which gives 49 × 49 = 2401
secondary sub-kingdoms in the first elemental
kingdom, and 7203 in all in the three elemental kingdoms. We cannot enter into all the details of the types of consciousness working in all these divisions, but the occult teaching says:—" The Monad contains within itself in latency the power of answering to any rate of vibration set up in its outer casings by an external stimulus. Differences of rates of vibrations thus set up lead to internal divisions. Thus one becomes many, and the many are born into the world of form."

We need not enter into the wonderful details of how forms have come up through the mineral, vegetable, and animal kingdoms to man, though
The Recording Angels we are told that the bodies of animal-men were built by Nature-spirits under the influence of Jupiter. At each re-birth the Ego attracts to itself the elemental essence of the Kingdoms. That we may have to deal with later; but as regards the building of the physical body there is the great question of the Recording Angels to consider. If we could trace the work of the various elementals connected with the building of our bodies we should learn much that would help us in our astrological studies, for the great consciousness of God is flowing through all the kingdoms of nature, and we are limited in our

LECTURE II. 53

expression of His life or consciousness by the sheaths or bodies we possess.

Only five planes out of the seven are concerned at present in our evolution, and only five Rulers, Angels, or planets are astrologically recognised **Only Five** if we exclude the Sun and Moon in the **out of Seven** ordinary older list of seven. These Gods or Rulers of planes are Indra, Vāyu, Agni, Varuna and Kubera, counting from above downwards. Although we cannot enter upon the vast field of enquiry into all the details of the Gods or Devas and of the matter in which they work, we should understand that we may find a useful correspondence between the planetary spheres, these Devas, the Rays, and the states of consciousness. Dealing with the Solar System we find a correspondence with occult teaching in the following:

☉	*Akâsha*	INDRA	Spirit
☿	*Airy Triplicity*	VAYU	Spiritual Soul
♀ ⎫			⎧ Human Soul
♄ ⎬	*Fiery* ,,	AGNI	⎨ (bridge between)
☽ ⎭			⎩ Animal Soul
♂	*Watery* ,,	VARUNA	Passions
♃	*Earthy* ,,	KUBERA	Life Principle
			Physical

It may be necessary to state that *these correspondences are not permanent;* also that they are interchangable, through the various sub-divisions, already mentioned. For instance, the airy and fiery triplicities are interchangable as are also the earthy and watery. It is not possible to take a single influence below the seven planetary spirits that is not interblended with another. The seven planetary spirits are one in the Sun, and are ever seeking that unity through their manifestations.

There are only three realities for us at all times to remember; the *Self*, the *Not Self*, and the *relation between them*. The Self is ever identifying Itself with the not-Self, and repudiating it, on all planes. In the table just given the Sun, Mercury, and Venus represent the Higher Self on the Higher planes and are :

Three Realities only

☉ Being, knowing itself as such on the Akāshic level as Atmā, the true Self in manifestation ;

☿ is the spiritual Soul or wisdom on the plane of Vayu or the intuitional.

♀ is the self-conscious human soul or intellect on the plane of Agni, the mental.

♄ is the bridge of knowledge between the Higher Self and its reflection in the Lower Self.

Saturn also stands for the physical man as a complex being compounded of animal and human, and as such Saturn separates the dross of the lower and refines the sheaths of the man through sacrifice.

In the Lower Self THE MOON is a reflection of the Sun, and as such represents the lower concrete mind, as a *mixture* of the animal and the man, and so termed the " Personality," the mind or instinctual soul of the animal-man.

Reflections

LECTURE II.   55

MARS reflects the intuitional wisdom of Mercury and in the lower world translates it as emotion, sympathy, feeling, desire and passion, through the plane of Varuna, God of Waters. JUPITER then takes up the whole of the Being, and on the physical plane shows forth the *Self* on the lowest rung of the living ladder of life.

From the foregoing we should now understand something of Jupiter's influence as the greater benefic on the physical plane. There is no **Constant Change** *permanent* physical body, since every part of the body is in a constant flux or change. The bones, the most solid part of the body, are under SATURN, and the lymph under THE MOON and VENUS. The muscles as agents of movement under MARS, and the nervous system under MERCURY. The *blood*, the nutritive system, and cell development, the most adaptable parts of the body are under Jupiter; and the "prana" or vitality or physical life is specialised under the organising influence of JUPITER and THE SUN.

When the Central Invisible (the Lord Ferho) saw the efforts of the divine *Scintilla*, unwilling to be dragged lower down into the degradation of matter, to liberate itself, he permitted it to shoot out from itself a *monad*, over which, attached to it as by the finest thread, the Divine Scintilla (the soul) had to watch during its ceaseless peregrinations from one form to another. Thus the monad was shot down into the first form of matter and became encased in stone; then, in course of time, through the combined efforts of *living fire* and *living water*, both of which shone their *reflection* upon the stone, the monad crept out of its prison to sunlight as a lichen From change to change it went higher and higher; the monad, with every new transformation borrowing more of the radiance of its parent, Scintilla, which approached it nearer at every transmigration.

Paraphrased from the " Book of Splendor" :

ISIS UNVEILED : i 302.

LECTURE III.

SYNOPSIS.—Jupiter and the Personal Aura —The connection of Jupiter with Substance and the Material World.
CONCLUSION: The Planetary Rays.

The Aura
Just as the earth is surrounded by an atmosphere, which is bright, clear, dull, or cloudy, according to the planetary vibrations, so is every human being enveloped in the AURA, which also is affected by planetary vibrations that are in harmony or discord with the nativity. It is unnecessary to enter into elaborate details concerning the gradations and colours of the Aura, as this will be found fully described in *Man Visible and Invisible*, where many coloured illustrations are given showing the conditions of the aura, from that of the savage state to the splendid aura of the perfect man.

Its Colours
Mrs Besant also has described the aura and its colours in one of the "People's Books" published by Messrs. Jack & Co., in a sixpenny edition, entitled *Theosophy*, from which the following is an extract: "The clarity, delicacy and brilliance of the auric colours, or their opacity, coarseness, and dullness, show the general state of advancement of the owner. Changes of emotion suffuse the astral portion with transitory colours, as with the rose

of love, the blue of devotion, the grey of fear, the brown of brutality, the sickly green of jealousy. The pure yellow of intelligence, the orange of pride, the brilliant green of mental sympathy and alertness, are equally familiar. Striations, bands, streaks, flashes, all expressive of certain qualities in the mental and moral character. The child's aura again differs much from that of the adult. . . . "

The human aura as the original and ultimate vehicle of the spiritual soul, termed by St. Paul the " celestial body," is thought to be mainly **The Celestial Body** under the *preserving* influence of the planet Jupiter through all the sub-influences of that planet on the various planes of manifestation. Jupiter's cyclic period of twelve years through the circle of the zodiac has a close correspondence with the diurnal and annual motion of the earth round the Sun; and Jupiter is practically a miniature Sun to our physical globe, for it is believed to rule over dimensional space with the tendency to preserve the harmony of our spheres while increasing and expanding the substance in which our earth is moving through space

Students of Astro-Meteorology are aware that Jupiter's stationary equatorial, or tropical positions tend to raise the temperature, and, when aspecting **Jupiter's influence** the Sun alone, to cause fine and **on the weather** mild weather. In the springtime Jupiter's influence on the atmosphere

LECTURE III. 59

has a softening effect, bringing pleasant winds and mild air, causing the sap in shrub and tree to rise and expand; and again in autumn the air is warm, tending to mellow the leaves on the trees as they fall, adding beauty to the autumnal changes in nature. Jupiter's influence on the atmosphere produces the clouds resembling mountains of wool known as the "cumulus" clouds, which diminish in the sky as Jupiter gains the ascendancy over disturbing conditions and accumulate when that planet is affected by contrary influences such as those of Saturn, and which are liable to produce thunder when aspected by Mars. A beautifully fine warm day and a very serene air may be foretold whenever Venus and Jupiter combined are the ruling aspects. Repeated observations prove that Jupiter in aspect with Mars in summer time increases the heat and tends to culminate in thunderstorms.

Each planet has its own electrical effect upon the atmosphere, producing natural causes that may be observed and understood by a careful study **Breathing** of astrology. Every breath we draw into our lungs is charged with electricity, which is concentrated ether. The air we breathe cannot pass below the lungs, but the ether it carries passes on into the nervous system and the vital organs. The science of breathing teaches many facts that explain the action of the planetary vibrations upon our sensitive etheric or lunar body.

The energy in our bodies is derived from a compression of the ether which is converted into electrical currents affecting every part of the body as represented by the twelve signs of the zodiac. Breathing is produced by the expansion (♃) and contraction (♄) of the lungs (♊), diaphragm (♉), and abdomen (♍). It is not the air we breathe that contains the electric energy or vitality, but the ether that is concealed in it, which, once in the body, cannot escape owing to insulation of the tissue. The lung breath is under the influence of MERCURY, and the ether or vital breath under the planet JUPITER. These two planets preside over those signs forming the Mutable Cross. From the Divine Intelligences we obtain the dynamic force which we call life. Aries, Leo and Sagittarius represent three stages of dynamic life as it animates the physical body, which we may classify as mental, emotional and physical energy.

The cosmic or universal life rays of the Sun are specialised through Jupiter, as "prana," or etheric vitality and transmitted through the Moon to the lunar body. The Cardinal Cross in the zodiac symbolises the functional organs in the physical body, and in the sign Cancer JUPITER has exaltation. The Fixed Cross symbolises the permanent or vital centres in the body (Ezekiel's wheel), in which THE MOON is exalted in the sign Taurus. And the Mutable Cross

LECTURE III. 61

symbolises the human soul and acts as a medium or relation between the permanent centres and the changeable vehicles. The vital principle animates the mutable signs through the channel of the breath. The lung breath is governed through Gemini and the vital breath in the spinal column through Sagittarius; the solar plexus through Virgo, and the tissues through Pisces.

When in India, we were invited to attend some sports at the Central Hindu College, where we saw a strong man perform a few strange feats of strength. Virgo— After taking several deep breaths this man laid himself down upon the ground and had placed on his abdomen several large slabs of granite, on the top of which several men stood for a few minutes. It looked a dangerous feat but we were assured that the performer suffered no inconvenience, for he knew the science of breathing, and had filled his solar plexus with ether. The solar plexus is under the sign Virgo, the sign of circulation. Its opposite sign is Pisces, which we fully believe has some relation to the beginnings of protoplasmic life drawn from the ethers of space.

The symbol of the sign Pisces is two half circles united by a cord or thread, symbol of the electric current of life. It is pictorially represented by —and Pisces two fishes swimming in opposite directions, which we are inclined to interpret as one half of the cell-life it denotes tending to involution by compression, and the other half to evolution by expansion. It is the "mystery sign" of the zodiac and behind its symbology there lies that which is yet to be revealed. In its highest interpretation it is the sign of the Universal Solvent, in which all things are dissolved and reformed, the sign in which the world saviours are said to be born, and its connection with its complementary sign Virgo, the sign of the immaculate conception, suggests the birth of the soul through the ethers of space; and when these are conveyed through the air in the lungs into the solar plexus there is a living incarnation of the higher life. When the Pharisees sought a sign of Jesus, He said, "There shall no sign be given but the sign of the prophet Jonas:" *Matt.* xvi., 4. This has been interpreted as the Sun reborn in the sign Pisces.

It is in the sign Pisces, the last sign of the Zodiac, that the human star of redemption is said to shine forth, which is probably the planet Venus, exalted in this sign, representing the pure or intuitive mind, *manas*. Pisces, the most paradoxical sign of the zodiac, may well be the mystery sign of life and form, it is the sign of outborn aquatic or protoplasmic life. We are not seeking to restrict the cell, or protoplasmic, life to the sign Pisces but to show its connection with the planet Jupiter and the germs of life that bud and blossom in the human aura. We do, however, believe that the origin of the simplest forms of life may be traced to this sign, which is truly a sign of "bubbles" in more senses than one.

LECTURE III. 63

In the Fourth of the seven existing Creative Orders, reflected in the earth's zodiac, we find SATURN as the guardian of the human monads who are now ♄ — ♃ struggling on the cross of matter, and in the Seventh, (or twelfth of the original order), we find the planet JUPITER presiding over the hosts of Devas, nature-spirits, and elementals connected with the lowest kingdoms and having to do with the building of the body of man; and if we follow closely the teaching concerned with the elemental kingdoms we shall find that Jupiter, and in all probability in some more material sense the sign Pisces, has to do with the "spirits of atoms" and the seeds of evolution of future kingdoms.

A careful study of the *Secret Doctrine* would lead us to believe that Jupiter is the planet that denotes the high water mark in our human evolution. The angels (or Devas to use the correct term) working under the influence of Jupiter, guide physical evolution; in each Round of the earth they prepare the forms and give man his etheric double, or the pattern mould on which his physical and his auric bodies are built; and they preside over his past, present and future. In some respects Jupiter may appear to be a paradoxical planet; for instance, it is said to rule over the physical body in its purely human aspects, and the vitality or prana flowing through the body, while it is also said that the Sun gives the vitality,

The High-Water Mark

and that no planet other than the earth actually governs the physical body, owing to its impermanence. It is true that the physical body is not under any *permanent* ruling of the planets, since all the planetary influences converge in the physical, or to be more strictly accurate, in the etheric part of the body.

The whole subject of the planetary and zodiacal influence is so vast and extensive that it is impossible to deal with them successfully in one Course of Lectures, and this causes many statements to seem fragmentary, —which they necessarily must be until the principles of the whole scheme of evolution are fairly mastered. The symbology of the planetary influence was therefore the subject of our first lecture, in which it was shown that the Sun symbolised by ☉ represents Spirit and life. The Moon ☽ soul and mind. And the earth or cross + body and matter. Spirit and life require an appropriate vehicle for expression, otherwise they would be unmanifest. Spirit and life are universal, the Sun shines on all alike. Life is specialised in plant and animal, and belongs to the plant or animal so long as the *form* holds it. The Moon is the Mother of all simple or innocent forms that are common to our earth, and it influences the lowest ethers by giving shape to those forms that are archetypally pictured in the zodiac; but the forms in themselves are colourless and are merely moulds or pattern models. The earth or the cross

A vast subject

LECTURE III.   65

hardens and makes concrete all forms through the axes of growth, symbolised by the cross and its relation to the circle. It is the earth that contains all the elements compounded in the physical form, but these elements are only held together by the influence of the planetary vibrations, which bind or loosen the compounds.

It is said quite truly that the element in the earthy triplicity is perceived through the sense of smell, and the other senses are also perceived in the triplicities such as water, taste; air, touch; fire, sight; and the whole zodiac, hearing;—although *hearing* has also a special relation with earth by downward reflection, especially Capricorn.

F.E.A.W.

In the same way the Fixed signs represent the vital centres in the body, the Cardinal signs the functional system and the Mutable signs the mind or intellect; but the *whole* is expressed through the physical body by way of the etheric mould which contains all the elements of the zodiac latent in the etheric state, governed by THE MOON.

F.C.M.

The planetary vibrations are but modifications of the one infinite life and consciousness of God, and we climb out of matter and all the etheric limitations through these planetary vibrations which reveal an inner or esoteric meaning to the senses. The sense of taste for example is *not wholly physical* for it leads to a higher taste seen in a true sense of proportion, a taste for music, art, or

Higher Senses

literature, etc. In the same way the sight denoted by the fiery signs will reveal an inner sight as insight, inner perception, or clairvoyance, ending in seeing physical things with spiritual eyes, etc. The sense of touch may also be carried to an inner sensitiveness to surroundings and persons or ability to keep in touch with people or things mentally, psychically or spiritually. The crude physical senses find expression through the elements manifesting in the physical body by means of the sense organs, but the extension of those senses produces the psychic,—who becomes reliable only when he has *trained* the inner senses and has not allowed himself to be fascinated by them, as a glutton would be by the physical sense of taste.

Just as the whole circle of the zodiac is a sounding board in which all the senses are synthesised both physically and psychically, so we may assume **Smell** that in the co-ordinating of forms the planet Jupiter is the synthesising planet, for it governs all extension of form or sense, and rules over all the elementals and Devas, being literally the God over gods and men. We have said that Jupiter rules the blood in animals and men. There is a peculiar smell in the blood well known to specialists, and that smell is an emanation from the protoplasmic life belonging to a particular animal or man. The protoplasmic life is the same for all beings, but the smell concealed in it specialises with the specialised life; and there is also a peculiar scent above

LECTURE III.   67

and beyond the smell, which decides the quality of the being. Every human being gives off from his body a peculiar odour or scent which is different from any other odour and arises out of the quality or condition of the blood. If we could discover the colour and property of the etheric conditions in the body we should be able at once to trace it to the sub-influence of the planets' vibrations working under the major influence of Jupiter on the form side of existence. JUPITER as ruler of the Aura embraces the whole of the planetary vibrations, and synthesises them through THE MOON or etheric body in the physical,—as well as preserving the aroma or subtle perfume of the merit extracted from the mental, emotional and physical uses made of those vibrations, which are stored in the whole of the human-aura.

The mortal part of man's nature is all that manifests below the finer vibrations of SATURN representing the purified nature or highly moral character in which the individual self is turned toward the spiritual life. That which is immortal is represented by MERCURY, VENUS and JUPITER from the standpoint of their creative influences. The vital life of THE SUN, common to all beings, is reflected and modified by THE MOON and unites with the higher ether represented by JUPITER and is then known as "prana," or specialised human life in the blood. It is the influence of JUPITER that decides the environment and future physical condi-

Lord of the Future

68 JUPITER: THE PRESERVER

tions of every soul whether animal, human, or divine, and it is *this influence* that is used by the recording angels when they decide the destiny of the re-incarnating ego. It is this influence that preserves the records of the past and shows the possibilities of the future. When a child is first born the *aura* in which it has to grow is almost pure white, and in it lie the potentialities of all the other planets as sub-influences of the presiding Jupiter. The details connected with the aura at the birth of a child are too elaborate to deal with at present. But it may be stated that the auric egg of every human being is the transmitter from the periodical lives to the life eternal. The periodic lives are represented by the influence of MARS, THE MOON, and the COMMON SOLAR LIFE— plus a portion of Jupiter's influence specialised as "prana." The immortal or eternal life is represented by the higher vibrations of SATURN, stability or permanence; VENUS, intuition; and MERCURY, memory; plus the finest film of substance—Jiva,—under the influence of JUPITER, who is the Preserver of all the psyche that passes over the Bridge of Saturn.

While the use of the word "prana" conveys so much meaning to the esoteric student, it is not easily understood by other students. Jiva is the real life of the soul; it becomes "prana" the moment a child breathes in the physical atmosphere. There are seven degrees in the aura, but the whole is under the preserving

The word "prana"

LECTURE III. 69

influence of Jupiter; prana is practically the lowest degree. The Moon and the ascending degree of the zodiac at birth represent the physical body, but without Jupiter's influence there is no expansive *conscious* life. The idea has been ably expressed by the simile of a sponge immersed in water. The water in the sponge's interior may be compared to " prana ": outside is Jiva. prana is the motor principle in life. The " lives " leave prana ; prana does not leave them. Take the sponge out of water and it becomes dry, thus symbolising death. Every principle is a differentiation of Jiva, the universal cosmic life, but the life motion in each is Prana, the breath of life.

Jupiter, Prana, and the Aura are the same, but what is most important is the influence of the planetary vibrations upon the aura as a whole; for we then discover that while the planets are outside us they are also within us, by their vibrations, and by the preservation of them through the majestic influence of Jupiter the planet of dimensional space causing curves in the aura marking off one division from another.

The Planets *within* us

When judging a nativity we do not as a rule look particularly to the planet Jupiter to discover anything special about a child or grown-up person; we note first the Sun, Moon, and Ascendant,—

Judging Responsiveness

and rightly so since they are the general indicators showing life common to all through the solar influence, and the instincts inherent in all through the lunar influence, and the disposition or personal conditions signified by the ascendant. But when we have satisfied ourselves as to the general conditions, then we begin to specialise in order to know the responsiveness and budding possibilities of the particular individual we are measuring, (either by the ordinary rules of astrology or our own intuition). If we have no inclination to study the deeper side of Astrology, it is of little use going into the details necessary for a closer study. To some students it may be that the physical body is the beginning and end of all investigation, but that superficial study will not satisfy those students who remember that the physical body is but a collection of cells drawn from living physical matter to serve as an instrument for objective perception through contacting the physical world.

If it is true that every body has its own peculiar smell, and the majority of students must admit that it has, then we shall require to know **Smell and Taste** under which planetary influence to place it. The rudiments of all our senses are contained in the ethers, which manifest in us through the blood under the peculiar rhythmic vibration of Jupiter and find their outlet in the physical body through the elements presiding over the zodiacal tripli-

LECTURE III.   71

cities of signs, the Earthy Triplicity producing the sense of smell, the nose being the corresponding organ in the physical body. The earthy triangle is composed of Taurus, Virgo, Capricorn, linked by opposite or complementary vibrations to the watery triplicity Scorpio, Pisces, Cancer. The planet JUPITER placed in any one of these six signs gives a distinctive scent or smell to the body born at that time, the most pronounced arising out of the sign Cancer in which the planet Jupiter is exalted. The Watery Triplicity yields the sense of taste and when THE MOON, ruler of the watery signs synthesised in Cancer, is in the sign Taurus, her exaltation, the senses of taste and smell are especially well developed. The sense of smell awakens objective perception, as the sense of taste awakens the instinctual perceptions. The most sensuous Taureans delight in scent and perfume, and they can be the most lustful of people when the physical senses alone appeal to their passional natures. The complementary nature of the earthy and watery signs should be known and understood.

We cannot now enter into the details connected with each sign of the zodiac and the senses, but we wish to show that the sense of smell cannot be
Connections confined to dense physical matter but that it is, in common with the other senses, related to the ethers of space, over which Jupiter presides as a preserving agent retaining in the aura around the physical body the fundamental activities of each of the

senses. We may trace the aura in four of its divisions by relating them to the physical senses and the inner planes of being. The earthy signs and the Moon may thus be related to the etheric or health aura, forming a radiation of its own and connected with Jupiter through ♍-♓, the solar plexus and the blood. The astral aura is connected by the watery signs, linking the Moon and Jupiter through the sign Cancer. The sense of sight and the fiery signs connect the mental aura through Jupiter and the sign Sagittarius, which represents magnetic perceptions. Finally the celestial body, represented by a combination of the fiery and the airy triplicity, is connected with Jupiter through the sign Gemini governing the lungs through which the air passes, transferring the ether it contains to the solar plexus. The airy signs are related to the sense of touch and link the soul with the body through the psycho-physiological perceptions. The higher bodies in the aura are related to VENUS and MERCURY where Jupiter has less physical and more spiritual influence.

Had we the time to dwell upon the significance of the Mutable cross in relation to the Fixed and Cardinal we should show how the whole circle of the zodiac is linked up sign by sign through the planet Jupiter, but it will be sufficient to point out that, commencing from the Sun sign Leo, the mutable signs come between the fixed and cardinal all the way round

One Stupendous Whole

LECTURE III. 73

the twelve signs. The main idea, however, we wish to establish is that the transmutation of the air we breathe through the lungs, ♊, extracts, by means of an expansion beyond the lungs, the ether concealed in the air; and this ether, *which is in more than one state of potency*, passing through the diaphragm to the solar plexus, ♍, is the vital essence which makes us the intelligent beings we are. The fact that esoteric students must realise, is the existence of *ONE ELEMENT* out of which arise six SUB-ELEMENTS, from whose essence comes Man whether physically, psychically, mentally, or spiritually considered. Four of these sub-elements we may trace to the senses connected with the triplicities in the zodiac, the whole being synthesised in the planet Jupiter, the Great Lord over all the elements.

We claim that the planet Jupiter stands at the head of the elements and is, therefore, the greater benefic as all astrologers have claimed **The Greater Benefic** him to be. This is why Jupiter presides over all ceremonies, and unless his aid is invoked all magical rites and effectual manifestations are useless. He is the lord of incantation, mantrams, sacred fires and the incense connected with religious ceremonies. Every force that we term magnetic, sympathetic, antipathetic, nervous, occult, dynamic, mental or mechanical,—in fact all force, is derived from the invisible ethers of space, planetary

JUPITER: THE PRESERVER

vibrations being nothing more nor less than the expression of the One Element in its manifold sub-divisions. When more is known concerning that unchangeable and indestructible fluid which is now termed "ether" in which the whole universe is floating, we shall trace every planetary vibration we are now classifying in physical terms, to that ILLIMITABLE ETHER which now forms the space in which we see the millions of stars around us. *We do not feel the motion of the earth's orbital revolution*, the atmosphere around it moving silently through the ether round the Sun. In the same way as the earth is enveloped in an atmosphere encased in the ether, so are we enveloped in an atmosphere which we term our personal magnetism, and this again is encased in an aura concerning which we are *just as unconscious* as we are regarding the ether of Space. And yet that aura comprises our personal world.

To live consciously in it and understand its possibilities we must extend the five physical senses beyond the limitations of their organs, and **Superconsciousness** realise that they may all be synthesised under the most psychic of all the planets, the planet Jupiter, who presides at the beginning and the ending of our individual existence; for when we know all that Jupiter's influence can teach us we shall find that superconsciousness which will give us our place among the Gods.

LECTURE III.

We have now traced the influence of Jupiter and the meaning of its symbol, first in relation to other symbols (Lecture I.), and then from a wider and grander (cosmic) point of view in our second Lecture, and lastly we have turned our attention to the influence of Jupiter in the aura of man himself, studying the matter thus from three standpoints,—metaphysical, cosmical, and personal. A few words on what are known as the Planetary Rays must now bring this Course of Lectures to a close.

(Marginal note: Metaphysical, Cosmical, Personal.)

*Our birth is but a sleep and a forgetting;
The soul that rises with us, our life's star,
    Hath had elsewhere its setting,
    And cometh from afar:
    Not in entire forgetfulness,
    And not in utter nakedness,
But trailing clouds of glory do we come
    From God, who is our home.*

*Earth fills her lap with pleasures of her own;
Yearnings she hath in her own natural kind,
And, even with something of a mother's mind,
    And no unworthy aim,
    The homely nurse doth all she can
To make her foster-child, her inmate man,
    Forget the glories he hath known,
And that imperial palace whence he came.*

CONCLUSION

THE PLANETARY RAYS

Although very little is now actually known with regard to the "Rays" along which the human family is evolving, there is very little doubt that Astrology will ultimately throw more light upon their influence than any other study.

The *Secret Doctrine*, from which the writer has drawn so much inspiration, contains a great deal of information that suggests an intimate relationship between the "Rays" and the planetary spheres of influence. In the Stanzas we are taught the ONE Ray is the Logos of our Solar System who is a Ray from the *ONE* on the unreachable plane of ABSOLUTE-NESS and INFINITY, upon which no speculation is possible. From the Solar Logos emanate the seven Rays or creative powers.

The Stanza says:—THE ONE RAY MULTIPLIES THE SMALLER RAYS. LIFE PRECEDES FORM, AND LIFE SURVIVES THE LAST ATOM (of Form—*external body*). THROUGH THE COUNTLESS RAYS THE LIFE-RAY, THE ONE, PROCEEDS, LIKE A THREAD THROUGH MANY BEADS. The teaching is clear that the Rays are the "Seven Sons of Light," also called "Stars," as is also the statement that:—"The Star under which a human entity is born will forever remain its star throughout the series of its reincarnations in one lifecycle. But this is not his *astrological* star. The latter is concerned and connected with the *Personality*; the former with the INDIVIDUALITY. The 'Angel' of that star will be the 'presiding' Angel so to speak, in every rebirth of the Monad, *which is part of his own essence*, though its vehicle, man, may remain forever ignorant of that fact. . . . ." (S.D. i. 626).

It is this INDIVIDUAL STAR that the true student of Astrology is seeking. And it is the writer's firm conviction, after many years of close study, that Astrology *in its esoteric interpretation* stands in the same relation to the true Astrology as the Darwinian theory of evolution does to the view of evolution taken by the student of Occultism. Instead of matter "evolving up" to spirit, the true evolution is an unfolding of the spiritual life concealed in matter. Yet the Darwinian theory of evolution was the herald of the loftier conceptions of Reincarnation and Karma. And in the same way Astrology, *as now generally understood*, is the forerunner of a higher teaching concerning the "Rays" which guide and govern evolution in all its many phases.

The *Secret Doctrine* contains what amounts to a direct prophecy in this direction, when it states that "our destiny *is* written in the Stars! Only, the closer "the union between the mortal reflection Man and his "celestial PROTOTYPE, the less dangerous his external "conditions and subsequent reincarnations. For there

LECTURE III. 79

"are *external* and *internal* conditions which affect the
"determination of our will upon our actions, and though
"man cannot escape his *ruling* Destiny, he has the
"choice of two paths, and it is in his power to follow
"either. Those who believe in Karma have to believe
"in Destiny, which, from birth to death, man is weaving
"around himself as a spider weaves his web; and this
"destiny is guided either by the heavenly voice of the
"invisible Prototype, or by our intimate *astral* or inner
"man, who is but too often our evil genius. Both of
"these lead on the outward man, and from the beginning
"the implacable *law of compensation* steps in and takes
"its course. When the last strand is woven, man finds
"himself completely under the empire of this *self-made*
"destiny, and this is KARMA": (S.D. i, 700).

Naturally the question will be asked: How is man to find his Individual Star? The answer is simply stated, and is not difficult to understand by those who desire understanding. We must begin acting from *within* instead of ever following impulses from *without,* namely those produced by our physical senses and gross physical body.

The exoteric astrologer looks to the stars without himself, the esoteric astrologer looks for the Star within, following the teaching of Him whose Star the Wise Men saw in the East, Who said that the kingdom of Heaven is within us, finally declaring that He and His Father Star were one, and that we were His brethren.

80 JUPITER: THE PRESERVER

NOTE BY THE ACTING EDITOR
OF " MODERN ASTROLOGY."

London, N.W., 11/9/1917

A special interest attaches to this book inasmuch as it was the last Mr Leo wrote. The first proofs were read by him a few days before his death.

He was at that time engaged upon a complete revision and reorganisation of the "system" of delineation which he had developed to such a high degree of effectiveness, and which had stood the test of practical application for over a decade and a half—briefly presented in *The Key to Your Own Nativity*.

The special feature of this revised system is, I understand, that the 'predictive' element is absent. At the moment of writing I have had no opportunity of examining it and can give no further description.

From the last communication I received from him, dated 27/8/17 (three days before his death) I learned that Mr Leo intended to write another chapter in order that this book might contain about the same number of pages as its predecessors in the series. This his death has prevented, and it is left for me to determine what is to be done. Nor have I much time in which to come to a decision: already the book is late, and the wholesale dealers are complaining

NOTE BY THE EDITOR

of the delay—the very proofs which were posted to Mr Leo a few hours after his death have lain for ten days uncorrected owing to the necessity for seeing to funeral and business arrangements, etc., and no opportunity is therefore afforded me for going quietly through his manuscripts and selecting what might suggest itself as most suitable.

In these circumstances it has seemed to me that the last article he wrote, (which the Hon. Sec. of the Astrological Society has kindly allowed me to reprint from the currrent issue of the Society's quarterly "Notes"), is not only likely to be acceptable to the reader but possesses the additional advantage of keeping well in train with the thought,—besides forming an apt corollary to the study of SATURN and JUPITER. For Saturn binds, while Jupiter releases: it is the Saturnine interpretation of Astrology which has led to such insistence, such undue insistence, upon the predictive element popularly known under the term "Directions." But it is the mission of Jupiter to bring home to the soul a realisation that the Stars incline, they do not compel. For as Mr Leo wrote in a recent letter: "We must now make a new watchword—MAN IS MASTER OF HIS DESTINY."

I have ventured to append a short article entitled "What is Astrology," which was included in the same issue over the signature "Aquarius," since it seems to follow in natural sequence.

JUPITER: THE PRESERVER

A WORD TO THE FEW.

To have it admitted that *Astrology is a Science*, to hear a King's Counsel say that he is staggered by the weight of evidence he has received, and to find a firm of well-known solicitors armed with an abundance of testimony as to the *bona fides* of an exponent of Astrology, all taking place in a London Police Court,[1] is not the least of the wonders connected with the astrological movement at the present time. The greatest wonder is that a body of earnest and sincere students of this subject should have been sufficiently unified to arouse the attention of those spiritual influences that always work in the atmosphere that is formed when two or three are gathered together in the Master's name. Those who are the most receptive to these influences know that any movement that can *survive* a severe and thorough shaking, is a sound movement. As President of the Astrological Society I have had sufficient evidence during the past three years that the astrological movement is going forward during the present century by leaps and bounds, and it is due to a majority of the members of the Astrological Institute and Society that this forward movement has been assured.

It is not generally known that there are "Dark Forces" as well as the "Light Forces" at work in the world, the former absorbing the collective influence of

---

[1] July 9th and 16th, 1917—see *Modern Astrology* for Sept., 1917.

the Stars that has been abused by selfish wills and the latter the Intelligent forces that reach a certain level forming an atmosphere into which the unselfish thoughts and feelings of men may be raised. In the constant interplay between these two forces there are periods when a crisis arises, usually when extremes meet and cause a storm that bursts over the heads of those strong enough to battle with it. The world crisis we are now going through, known as the great European War, was the great storm between the Dark and Light forces Might and Right liberated at the close of the Uranian and Neptunian cyclic opposition. Intermingled with the Light and the Dark are innumerable side issues; scientific, philosophic, political, and religious, they are the shading, the light pencillings, and the dark shadows. There is not a *thinking* man or woman in the world to-day who is not affected by the present great crisis and the more pronounced the thought the more certain will be the attraction to the Light or the Dark. It cannot be a question of indifference at the present time; that will not do: for indifference means a *non*-human interest, and the interests at stake at the present time are vitally *human*. Every student of Astrology, by his thought on the subject, has invoked the light or the dark influences during the past three years, for those years have been years of choice, and consciously or unconsciously we have been creating an atmosphere around ourselves that is *attracted* to the light or the dark. It

84   JUPITER: THE PRESERVER

has been a thought atmosphere tinged with a bias one way or the other, and it is not too metaphysical to say that we have either threaded our thought in our own Star-Angel's web of destiny and linked ourselves with a thread of that great Angel's intelligence, or woven a coarser strand of material thought with the darker forces who break those finer threads by stimulating the animal nature that is within us.

To the few, and we are not many at present, I should like to say that whether we associate ourselves or not with the astrological movement that is now going forward, it is destined to go forward with us or without us.

The torch that was lighted by an earnest prayer in the year 1890, and reinforced in 1895, has since then lighted many torches that are now burning brightly round the altar of astrological truth. Prior to those years that branch of Astrology known as Horary held the day. It was a form of divination for which Astrology was almost solely used by those who studied it, and I was told by one who used it extensively that it was the only form of Astrology worth knowing. Many horoscope delineations were given when the time of birth was unknown, on horary figures only, with the same interpretation.

Small wonder that Astrology used in this manner became a farce and was ridiculed by those who knew the facilities it gave the charlatan and the impostor! Steady and persistent reiteration, since those dates, of

A WORD TO THE FEW   85

the well-known dictum *Character is Destiny* has practically turned the tide away from Horary to that of Natal Astrology which has aroused a genuine personal interest, and what is more a firm belief in the theories of karma and reincarnation.

Now, after a quarter of a century of remarkable propaganda work we find that another of the weak sides of astrological practice has to go, that of indiscriminate prediction.

Yes, whatever may or may not be our beliefs or inclinations, as sure as Astrology *is* a science so sure must the predictive element make way for the new thought that EFFORT IS STRONGER THAN DESTINY.

It will shock some, amuse others, and arouse the interest of a few. It is the few whose thought power will be strong enough to show the world why the true astrologer, who believes in destiny, can also believe in the exercise of man's free will. It is not the will that is self-centred, but the will that WILLS to unite with the will of the Creator who designed and planned the Universe; the will that works *with* evolution and not against it.

This is the secret of the Light and Dark forces, the one wills to unite and harmonise itself *with* the many, the other seeks to disunite and hold its will *against* the many.

Every day is a Judgment day, and the few are now called to the seat of Astrological Judgment. The predictive side of Astrology must go until we learn how to

JUPITER: THE PRESERVER

unbind the fetters of fate by knowledge, and teach all men that they are not bound and that none other holds them to the wheel of fate but themselves!

What is Astrology?—The definition of Astrology has been attempted in a single phrase, by saying that Astrology is the soul of Astronomy. It may be of interest to take it as a key-thought to a few reflections on the meaning of " Astrology."

In order to do so, it is necessary to enquire into the meaning of the word *soul*. Soul has a dual function: in relation to the body it is active, directive; in relation to spirit it is passive, receptive.

If, then, we accept the phrase " soul of astronomy " as an adequate definition, we must not lose sight of this dual function.

Astronomy, we may say, deals with the machinery of the stars—their situations, movements, and the forces or levers by which they are operated. It may be termed sidereal mechanics.

Now an engineer is content to construct a machine of given dimensions which shall work in a known manner and acquit itself agreeably to certain specifications. His responsibility ends there. With the destination or utility of the said machine he is not concerned. And, pursuing the analogy, we may say that the astronomer is

A WORD TO THE FEW 87

satisfied when he has demonstrated the locations of the stars and planets, their movements, and the laws (or shall we say habits?) which govern these movements,—govern, that is to say, in the sense of making their operation predicable. At that point the function of the astronomer ceases. Just as a mechanic will make you a typewriter which is an efficient instrument, but is not in the least concerned with the advantages of shorthand or the desirability of spelling reform,—though these are intimately associated with the typewriter and its effect on the user,—so the astronomer, as such, is not concerned with the purposes of the stars, and the relation of the planets to human conduct.

And yet typewriters are made for use, locomotives are made for transport, dynamos are made for the generation of the electric current; and not merely as exercises in mechanical skill. In the same way astronomy may fairly be compared with mechanical engineering, as a *means* only to an end, not as an end in itself. The engineer is a useful, a necessary person: but he is not made a member of the Cabinet, he is not placed in charge of a war, he is not even put upon the captain's bridge. And in like manner astronomy has to be regarded as existing not for its own sake, but as the purveyor of useful material to those who know how to make use of that material.

That being granted, it may be postulated that astrology stands in a like relationship to astronomy as literature

88 JUPITER: THE PRESERVER

to the typewriter or as seamanship to the steam-engine. It is the user, the "captain on the bridge."

In this I think we shall all agree, namely that the ultimate purpose of astronomy is to serve astrology.

But if our aphorism "Astrology is the soul of Astronomy" contains a real truth, and if the dual function of the soul be admitted, (as I think on investigation it infallibly must), then it follows that astrology likewise must be the servitor of something higher, albeit we cannot at present determine what that something is. But to pursue our analogy one stage further, just as the engineer is the servitor of the captain, so is the captain the servant of the State. He is a part of the State, lives in it and exists by it, yet by his very vocation he is a servant of it.

In the same way it would seem that Astrology may be the servant of something higher and greater. We have no name for it, but we may call it the Spirit.

Quality Paperbacks From Samuel Weiser

TRANSITS AND PLANETARY PERIODS by Sepharial
Written specifically for students of astrology, this book considers the problem of transits, their continuity and duration, so that when all factors are logically considered, it becomes possible to make continuous forecasts of the trend of events. The cyclic recurrence of events—the law of periodicity—is used to illustrate the planetary cycles and periods.

THE FIXED STARS AND CONSTELLATIONS IN ASTROLOGY
by Vivian E. Robson
A systematized compilation of all that has been written about the stars and constellations as applied to astrology. Contents also includes material on the Lunar Mansions and the uses of rulerships of the fixed stars and constellations in magic and the making of talismans.

MAN AND THE ZODIAC by David Anrias
The material and sketches here are the result of many years' study and artistic observation by a student of the Adept, the Rishi of the Nilgiri Hills. The illustrations, done in 1938, are typical of the unmodified decanate types. Included also are a method of synchronizing the elements of the chart and a section on the conscious, unconscious, and superconscious as related to the twelve signs. Paper.

DICTIONARY OF ASTROLOGY by James Wilson
Arranged in the alphabetical order of a true dictionary, this lexicon is comprehensive and easy to use. Prime authorities are cited in the enumeration and explanation of the various systems of astrology and in the extensive treatment of such subjects as directions, progressions, transits, and horary astrology. An indispensable reference work.

THE BOOK OF THOTH by The Master Therion (Aleister Crowley)
A complete and coherent picture of the Magical Path as shown in the Tarot pack. This is the first and final classic of Tarot, the key to all Western disciplines, and is indispensable to all who seek to fathom the deepest wisdom of the ancients and to follow the Initiated Tradition from the beginnings of History to the present day. 8 color illustrations, 90 in black and white. New York, 1969. 290 pages.

MAGIC WHITE AND BLACK by Franz Hartmann, M.D.
Magic is the divine art or exercise of spiritual powers by the awakened spirit in man to control invisible living elements and his own soul. The author shows that these spiritual powers must be developed before they can be exercised and explains the conditions necessary for this development. New York, 1970.

APPRENTICED TO MAGIC by W. E. Butler
Written specifically for the true aspirant atfer magical attainment, this book, if properly read, meditated upon and followed up, will bring those who are ready to the Doors of the Mysteries. It is written in the first person singular, taking the form of a series of personal instructions from a *guru* to his *chela*. London, 1969. 105 pp.

QABBALAH by Isaac Myer
The Philosophical Writings of Solomon Ben Yehudah Ibn Gebirol or Avicebron and their connection with the Hebrew Qabbalah and Sepher ha-Zohar with translations of selected passages as well as An Ancient Lodge of Initiates translated from the Zohar and an abstract of an essay upon the Chinese Qabbalah contained in the Yih King. Limited edition of 500 copies.

TURBA PHILOSOPHORUM translated with notes by Arthur Edward White
The "Assembly of the Sages" as this work is sub-titled is perhaps the most ancient extant treatise on alchemy in the Latin language. This is a translation into English with notes and index by an outstanding scholar.

ALCHEMICAL WRITINGS OF EDWARD KELLY
This translation from the Hamburg edition of 1676 contains treatises on the philosopher's stone and the theatre of terrestrial astronomy and is illustrated with "emblematic figures."

THE SECRET TRADITION IN ALCHEMY by Arthur Edward Waite
The development and records of this secret tradition from supernatural life, Hermetic mystery, Byzantine Alchemy, Arabian and Syriac Alchemy, the various alchemists and finally the analysis of the mystic side of alchemy.

BREATH AND THE ZODIAC by Sibyl Ferguson
Breath is the indispensable requisite to maintaining life and the zodiac sign, determined at birth, is inescapable. Considering these two factors together the character can be determined and improved. For each sign are given individualized exercises and affirmations; advanced steps in cyclic breath, success breath, etc., are also included. Paper.

ASTROLOGY OF THE ANCIENT EGYPTIANS by Karma
A study of this book will enable the student to erect a horoscope, an actual blueprint of the heavens at the time of birth, which will reveal the entire scope of a life. Based on the knowledge of the ancient Egyptians, this work goes back to the source of the ancient science of astrology.

THE PRE-NATAL EPOCH by E. H. Bailey
Rectification of recorded birth times and the calculation of the time of birth from past events with reference to, and checked by, Epochal Laws. Contains sections on: the scientific basis and laws of the epoch; the pre-natal epoch as a factor in single and multiple births; how to calculate a horoscope when the birth-time is unknown.

THE STARS by L. Edward Johndro
The author here sets out to show how the latitudinal position of the stars in any part of the heavens relates to personal or world events. The stars are considered as centers of radiant energy amplifying the tendencies of planets which configure with them. A valuable contribution to the limited material available on the fixed stars.

BOOK OF MEDIUMS by Allan Kardec
Here is the special instruction of the Spirits on the theory of manifestations; the means of communicating with the invisible world; the development of mediumship and the difficulties encountered in the practice of spiritism.

THE EARTH IN THE HEAVENS by L. Edward Johndro
Beginning with a detailed discussion of the precession of the equinox, both ecliptic and equatorial, he relates this precession to the midheavens and ascendants of cities and geographic points—there are tables for calculation and also a table of over 400 midheavens and ascendants for various cities. The uses of locality angles and the application of the longitudinal positions of the stars to nativities are also presented.